KWAME ANTHONY
APPIAH

This clear and engaging introduction is the first book to assess the ideas of Kwame Anthony Appiah, the Ghanaian-British philosopher who is a leading public intellectual today. The book focuses on the theme of 'identity' and is structured around five main topics, corresponding to the subjects of his major works: race, culture, liberalism, cosmopolitanism, and moral revolutions.

This helpful book:

- Teaches students about the sources, opportunities, and dilemmas of personal and social identity—whether on the basis of race, gender, sexuality, or class, among others—in the purview of Appiah.
- Locates Appiah within a broader tradition of intellectual engagement with these issues—involving such thinkers as W. E. B. Du Bois, John Stuart Mill, and Martha Nussbaum—and, thus, how Appiah is both an inheritor and innovator of preceding ideas.
- Seeks to inspire students on how to approach and negotiate identity politics in the present.

This book ultimately imparts a more diverse and wider-reaching geographic sense of philosophy through the lens of Appiah and his intellectual contributions, as well as emphasizing the continuing social relevance of philosophy and critical theory more generally to everyday life today.

Christopher J. Lee is an Associate Professor of History and Africana Studies at Lafayette College, USA.

ROUTLEDGE CRITICAL THINKERS

Series Editor: Robert Eaglestone, Royal Holloway, University of London, UK

Routledge Critical Thinkers is a series of accessible introductions to key figures in contemporary critical thought.

With a unique focus on historical and intellectual contexts, the volumes in this series examine important theorists':

- Significance
- Motivation
- Key ideas and their sources
- Impact on other thinkers

Concluding with extensively annotated guides to further reading, *Routledge Critical Thinkers* are the student's passport to today's most exciting critical thought.

Also available in the series:

Martin Heidegger
Timothy Clarke
Giorgio Agamben
Alex Murray
Frantz Fanon
Pramod K. Nayar
Paul Gilroy
Paul Williams
Mikhail Bakhtin
Alastair Renfrew
Hans-Georg Gadamer
Karl Simms
Karl Marx
Andrew Rowcroft
Kwame Anthony Appiah
Christopher J. Lee

For more information about this series, please visit: www.routledge.com/Routledge-Critical-Thinkers/book-series/SE0370

KWAME ANTHONY APPIAH

Christopher J. Lee

Routledge
Taylor & Francis Group

LONDON AND NEW YORK

First published 2021
by Routledge
2 Park Square, Milton Park, Abingdon, Oxon OX14 4RN

and by Routledge
605 Third Avenue, New York, NY 10158

Routledge is an imprint of the Taylor & Francis Group, an informa business

British Library Cataloguing-in-Publication Data
A catalogue record for this book is available from the British Library

Library of Congress Cataloging-in-Publication Data
Names: Lee, Christopher J., author.
Title: Kwame Anthony Appiah/Christopher J. Lee.
Description: Abingdon, Oxon; New York: Routledge, 2021. |
Series: Routledge critical thinkers | Includes bibliographical
references and index.
Identifiers: LCCN 2020053427 | ISBN 9780367223595 (hardback) |
ISBN 9780367229092 (paperback) | ISBN 9780429277559 (ebook)
Subjects: LCSH: Appiah, Anthony. | Identity (Psychology)
Classification: LCC B5619.G43 A675 2021 | DDC 126–dc23
LC record available at https://lccn.loc.gov/2020053427

ISBN: 978-0-367-22359-5 (hbk)
ISBN: 978-0-367-22909-2 (pbk)
ISBN: 978-0-429-27755-9 (ebk)

Typeset in Sabon
by Deanta Global Publishing Services, Chennai, India

CONTENTS

SERIES EDITOR'S PREFACE

The books in this series offer introductions to major critical thinkers who have influenced literary studies and the humanities. The *Routledge Critical Thinkers* series provides the books you can turn to first when a new name or concept appears in your studies.

Each book will equip you to approach a key thinker's original texts by explaining their key ideas, putting then into context and, perhaps most importantly, showing you why this thinker is considered to be significant. The emphasis is on concise, clearly written guides which do not presuppose a specialist knowledge. Although the focus is on particular figures, the series stresses that no critical thinker ever existed in a vacuum but, instead, emerged from a broader intellectual, cultural and social history. Finally, these books will act as a bridge between you and the thinkers' original texts: not replacing them but rather complementing what they wrote. In some cases, volumes consider small clusters of thinkers, working in the same area, developing similar ideas or influencing each other.

These books are necessary for a number of reasons. In his 1997 autobiography, *Not Entitled*, the literary critic Frank Kermode wrote of a time in the 1960s:

On beautiful summer lawns, young people lay together all night, recovering from their daytime exertions and listening to a troupe of Balinese musicians. Under their blankets or their sleeping bags, they would chat drowsily about the gurus of the time...What they repeated was largely hearsay; hence my lunchtime suggestion, quite impromptu, for a series of short, very cheap books offering authoritative but intelligible introductions to such figures.

There is still a need for 'authoritative and intelligible introductions'. But this series reflects a different world from the 1960s. New thinkers have emerged, and the reputations of others have risen and fallen, as new research has developed. New methodologies and challenging ideas have spread through the arts and humanities. The study of literature is no longer—if it ever was—simply the study and evaluation of poems, novels, and plays. It is also the study of ideas, issues and difficulties which arise in any literary text and in its interpretation. Other arts and humanities subjects have changed in analogous ways.

With these changes, new problems have emerged. The ideas and issues behind these radical changes in the humanities are often presented without reference to wider contexts or as theories which you can simply 'add on' to the texts you read. Certainly, there's nothing wrong with picking out selected ideas or using what comes to hand—indeed, some thinkers have argued that this is, in fact, all we can do. However, it is sometimes forgotten that each new idea comes from the pattern and development of somebody's thought and it is important to study the range and context of their ideas. Against theories 'floating in space', the *Routledge Critical Thinkers* series places key thinkers and their ideas firmly back in their contexts.

More than this, these books reflect the need to go back to the thinkers' own texts and ideas. Every interpretation of an idea, even the most seemingly innocent one, offers you its own 'spin', implicitly or explicitly. To read only books on a thinker, rather than texts by that thinker, is to deny yourself the chance of making up your own mind. Sometimes, what makes a significant figure's work hard to approach is not so much its style or the content as the feeling of not knowing where to start. The purpose of these books is to give you a 'way in' by offering an accessible overview of these thinkers' ideas and works and by guiding your further reading, starting with each thinker's own texts. To use a metaphor from philosopher Ludwig Wittgenstein (1889–1951), these books are ladders, to be thrown away after you have climbed to the next level. Not only, then, do they equip you to approach new ideas, but they also empower you, by leading you back to the theorists' own texts and encouraging you to develop your own informed opinions.

Finally, these books are necessary because, just as intellectual needs have changed, the education systems around the world—the contexts in which introductory books are usually read—have changed radically, too. What was suitable for the minority of higher education systems of the 1960s is not suitable for the larger, wider, more diverse, higher technology education systems of the 21st century. These changes call not just for new, up-to-date introductions but new methods of presentation as well. The presentational aspects of *Routledge Critical Thinkers* have been developed with today's students in mind.

Each book in the series has a similar structure. They begin with a section offering an overview of the life and ideas of the featured thinkers and explain why they are important. The central section of each book discusses the thinkers' key ideas, their context, evolution, and reception; in the books that deal with more than one thinker, the influence of each on the other is also explained and explored. The volumes conclude with a survey of the impact of the thinker or thinkers, outlining how their ideas have been taken up and developed by others. In addition, there is a detailed final section suggesting and describing books for further reading. This is not a 'tacked-on' section but an integral part of each volume. In the first part of this section, you will find brief descriptions of the thinkers' key works, and following this, information on the most useful critical works and, in some cases, on relevant websites. This section will guide you in your reading, enabling you to follow your interests and develop your own projects. Throughout each book, references are given in what is known as the Harvard system (the author and the date of a work cited are given in the text and you can look up the full details in the bibliography at the back). This offers a lot of information in very little space. The books also explain technical terms and use boxes to describe events or ideas in more detail, away from the main emphasis of the discussion. Boxes are also used at times to highlight definitions of terms frequently used or coined by a thinker. In this way, the boxes serve as a kind of glossary, easily identified when flicking through the book.

The thinkers in the series are 'critical' for three reasons. First, they are examined in the light of subjects which involve criticism: principally literary studies or English and cultural studies, but also other disciplines which rely on the criticism of books, ideas, theories, and unquestioned assumptions. Secondly, they are critical because studying their work will provide you with a 'toolkit' for your own informed reading and thought, which will make you critical. Third, these thinkers are critical because they are crucially important: they deal with ideas and questions which can overturn conventional understandings of the world, of texts, of everything we take for granted, leaving us with a deeper understanding of what we already knew and with new ideas.

No introduction can tell you everything. However, by offering a way into critical thinking, this series hopes to begin to engage you in an activity which is productive, constructive, and potentially life-changing.

ACKNOWLEDGMENTS

This critical introduction is the first book-length treatment of the philosophy of Kwame Anthony Appiah. It continues a series of books I have completed that address the social and historical dimensions of 'multiracial' identities in Africa. It also contributes to ongoing research I have pursued regarding decolonization and its histories. In this instance, I am interested in the question: Why the turn away from left radicalism, which defined many anticolonial movements, toward liberalism during the postcolonial period? Given the brevity of this Routledge series, I can only briefly touch upon an answer. However, I believe that Appiah is an important example of this generational shift toward liberal ideals, beginning in the 1970s.

A number of people have helped with this project. I want to thank the Connect Africa working group in the greater New York City area, with whom I shared a number of early ideas at the April 2019 workshop. I would like to thank in particular Mark Sanders, Ato Quayson, Jennifer Wenzel, Joseph Slaughter, and Stephanie Newell for their questions and responses. I wrote this book while a residential fellow at the Stellenbosch Institute for Advanced Study (2019) and at the Institute for Advanced Studies in the Humanities at the University of Edinburgh (2020). I would like to thank the staff at both for their support.

At Stellenbosch, I would like to further thank Uchenna Okeja and Dorian Bell for their insights. At Edinburgh, I would like to thank Emma Hunter, Charles West, Ania Grajek, and Rebekah Lee for accommodation and stimulating conversation. A number of people read the manuscript (or portions thereof) for which I am completely grateful. They include Bruce Janz, Esperanza Brizuela-Garcia, Carina Ray, Lindsay Ceballos, Lily Saint, Jeffrey Ahlman, Carol Summers, and Sarah Duff. Finally, I would like to extend my gratitude to Robert Eaglestone, Zoe Meyer, and Polly Dodson for their support and help with the editorial process at Routledge.

ABBREVIATIONS

All of the following publications are by Kwame Anthony Appiah.

WHY APPIAH?

Who are you? Who am I? How should we understand and relate to one another? These commonplace yet fundamental questions form the basis of Kwame Anthony Appiah's work. Identity is central to his scholarship, and identity is central to this book. Trained as a philosopher at Cambridge University, Appiah has concerned himself with a range of intellectual traditions, cultural histories, and scholarly approaches for addressing these essential questions that define our lives. Indeed, since receiving his doctorate in 1982, Appiah has achieved a level of fame that is rare among academic philosophers He has held appointments at a number of prestigious universities including Harvard, Princeton, Yale, the University of Ghana, and New York University, in addition to receiving public accolades such as delivering the Reith Lectures for the BBC in 2016 and serving as the Ethicist columnist for *The New York Times Magazine*. His books *Cosmopolitanism: Ethics in a World of Strangers* (2006) and *The Honor Code: How Moral Revolutions Happen* (2010) have been widely acclaimed bestsellers and translated into multiple languages.

However, the importance of Appiah extends beyond the interdisciplinary breadth of his writing and the reach of his ideas to both popular and scholastic audiences. Born in

London and raised in Kumasi, his body of work has bridged different parts of the world and their respective cultural traditions. In retrospect, his multiple senses of identification with Ghana, Britain, and the United States expressed in his scholarship, beginning in the 1990s, presaged popular themes in African fiction that has burst onto the literary scene since 2000. Critically acclaimed novels like *Americanah* (2013) by Chimamanda Ngozi Adichie, *Open City* (2011) by Teju Cole, *Ghana Must Go* (2013) by Taiye Selasi, and *Homegoing* (2016) by Yaa Gyasi have touched upon issues previously identified by Appiah, whether Afropolitanism in the Black Atlantic world or the historical challenges and political opportunities of identity in our frenetic global present. Like these works of fiction, Appiah's writing has frequently interrogated what it means to be 'African' and the dimensions of 'Blackness' more generally, whether in London, New York, or Lagos. Appiah is useful to think with in relation to these questions. Yet his arguments can be applied even more broadly. In a world riven with conflict over national, religious, racial, gendered, and other identities, Appiah has consistently posed the questions: What is 'identity', and how can a person's 'identity' provide a basis for living an ethical life?

These ordinary questions possess extraordinary implications. Consider, for example, the following sequence of global events during the past four decades since the start of Appiah's career: the collapse of the Soviet Union in December 1991; the Bosnian War from 1992 to 1995; the election of Nelson Mandela in South Africa in April 1994; the Rwandan Genocide from April to July 1994; the terrorist attack on the World Trade Center in New York in September 2001; and the police shooting of Michael Brown Jr. (1996–2014), an unarmed Black American teenager, in August 2014. Each of these moments demonstrates the powerful role that social identities play in our lives. They can foment political unrest and spark episodes of extreme violence, as in the cases of the Bosnian War and the Rwandan Genocide. Social identities can also shift and transform, as in the cases of South Africa and the Soviet Union. In the first case, racial differences were put aside, albeit temporarily, in favor of a new post-apart-heid South African identity. In the second case, the dissolution of the Soviet Union marked the denouement of a political iden-tity centered on Marxism-Leninism that had started with the Bolshevik Revolution in 1917. No one identifies as 'Soviet' any-more. And yet the experience of identity need not be national in origin or scale to be meaningful. The case of Michael Brown underscores how individuals confront the effects and vulnerabil-ities of certain identities and their legacies. His death and those of Trayvon Martin (1995–2012), Eric Garner (1970–2014), Sandra Bland (1987–2015), George Floyd (1973–2020), and Breonna Taylor (1993–2020), to name only a few, have become symbolic of racial injustice in the United States, inspiring grass-roots protests through the Black Lives Matter movement.

The case of Michael Brown is particularly instructive in rela-tion to Appiah's main arguments. For Appiah, it is essential to start at the level of the individual in order to approach, under-stand, and arrive at decisions about broader social conditions. Brown's death is tragic to his family in the first instance; it is also tragically emblematic of a systemic pattern of police bias and anti-Black violence in the US. Yet, it is important to appreciate and stress how individual lives are intersections of multiple iden-tities and circumstances. A central feature across Appiah's work is his skepticism toward group identities and how they can mis-represent and misguide individual experience, even with good intentions. More specifically, they can obscure and predetermine the ethical choices a person may make in ways that are detri-mental to her or him. Put simply, Appiah emphasizes the 'ethical self' in favor of the 'social self' that is rooted in group identity, even if the former is unavoidably influenced by the latter. As he puts it in *The Ethics of Identity* (2005),

A person's shaping of her life flows from her beliefs and from a set of values, tastes, and dispositions of sensibility, all of these influenced by various forms of social identity: let us call all these together a person's ethical self.

(EI: 163)

The topic of identity is not unique among philosophers. To pick two well-known examples, Jean-Paul Sartre (1905–80) and Simone de Beauvoir (1908–86) addressed this topic in *Anti-Semite and Jew* (1946) and *The Second Sex* (1949). Sartre and Beauvoir situated anti-Semitism and gender, respectively, within a phenomenological framework to analyze how identities are not biologically fixed, but socially made. Appiah can be placed within this broad tradition of inquiry. In his first major work, *In My Father's House: Africa in the Philosophy of Culture* (1992), Appiah addresses a sequence of key ideas including race, modernity, and Africa itself to underscore their illusory qualities, inconsistencies, and potential misdirection when applied to individual circumstances. Among his most recent books is *The Lies that Bind: Rethinking Identity* (2018), based on his BBC lectures, with the title itself extending his earlier arguments: we live by certain fictions of identity, whether these identities are based on religious belief, nation, or race. As he writes in *In My Father's House*, 'identities are complex and multiple and grow out of a history of changing responses to economic, political, and cultural forces, almost always in opposition to other identities' (IMFH: 178). He further adds that identities 'flourish despite … their roots in myths and in lies' (IMFH: 178). These arguments are unsettling and formidable: what we may feel most strongly about, what provides us with a sense of place, purpose, and community, and what can sustain us over the course of a lifetime may turn out to be untrue, or at least not completely true. Fictions can be more powerful than facts. Critical reasoning is essential for adjudicating the two.

This stance against the primacy of group identities has, at times, placed Appiah at odds with certain trends and perspectives, particularly with the social justice movements of our time. His emphasis on individual ethics over group politics—an approach which falls into a Western liberal political tradition—has been construed as too limited, even apolitical, by those who see identity as an enduring effect of systemic conditions rather than wholly a matter of individual choice. To be a member of the working class, to be a racial minority, or to be a member of a persecuted religion is not typically the result of personal decision. Appiah would agree. His more politically focused writing on moral revolutions in *The Honor Code*, which outlines the ways in which individuals have at times gone against their self-interest to bring widespread political change, addresses this critical perspective by speaking to the importance of broader social contexts. Though his arguments do not embrace an emancipatory politics in the vein of Karl Marx (1818–83) or Frantz Fanon (1925–61), Appiah does highlight the capacity of the individual through their own process of reasoning to contribute to and enable social transformation.

More to the point, Appiah does not conclude that it is foolish to embrace identity, that identities are ultimately meaningless. He is not *anti*-identity. Rather, his work aims to map a middle ground between the fictional attributes of social identities and their overdetermination—that is, Appiah equips his readers with the means for negotiating the contradictory nature of identity, whether in relation to themselves or in relation to others. This book outlines the critical method his scholarship has to offer. This method includes technical terms—such as 'extrinsic racism', 'intrinsic racism', and 'habitus' to name a few examples—for analyzing specific situations. This method can also be construed more broadly—the adoption of a skepticism that takes few things at face value. Identities are important for navigating social relations and the world as indicated at the start. But the embrace of singular identities at the expense of others can lead to forms of solipsism, discrimination, absolutism, and, at times, violence. Identity in its positive and its negative incarnations must be taken seriously.

This tension between embracing and critiquing identity is a reflection of Appiah's own struggles with the meaning of identity. As touched upon earlier, a compelling feature of his writing has been his consistent forthrightness in referencing his own life to illustrate the questions and predicaments with which he has grappled. Born in London to a British mother and a Ghanaian father, Appiah has lived between political and cultural worlds—Britain, Ghana, and the United States—as well as racial worlds through his 'multiracial' status. His Asante heritage, his Christian upbringing, and his Western education have all impacted his thinking. His sexuality as a gay man, which he has referenced only briefly in his work, is yet another layer of his personal identity that has placed him both on the margins and at the forefront of social and political contexts.

Amid this spectrum of communities, the solution for Appiah is not to choose one identity over the others. Rather, it is to learn how to inhabit multiple identities at once. As he explains in the preface to *In My Father's House*, a legacy he inherited from his father is the challenge and gift of manifold attachments—Asante, Ghanaian, African, Christian, and so forth. Appiah views this multiplicity as a source of abundance. This strength in liminality is further reflected in his interdisciplinary writing—between philosophy and literature, American studies and African studies, historical understanding and engagement with present debates and concerns. We might view this dualism as approximating the 'two standpoints' approach of the eighteenth-century German philosopher Immanuel Kant (1724–1804), who believed that the world can be approached through feeling—a 'sensible world' (*Sinnenwelt*)—as well as reason—the 'intelligible world' (*Verstandeswelt*)—as Appiah touches upon in *The Ethics of Identity* (EI: 55). Appiah ultimately practices a version of 'standpoint epistemology' (Harding 1992) by speaking from a personal history that has made identity an uneasy, complex, and enriching subject—at once tangible and tenuous, socially imposed yet also deeply felt.

HOW TO READ THIS BOOK

One might ask, then, what kind of philosopher is Kwame Anthony Appiah? As he writes in his textbook, *Thinking It Through* (2003), he often demurs when queried by acquaintances which philosophers he follows and if he has a 'philosophy' (TT: ix). Nonetheless, a key task of this book is to locate Appiah intellectually and historically. Both aspects are important for grasping the dimensions of his thought and work. His childhood in postcolonial Ghana and his education in Britain raise questions about how he can be situated within the disciplines of African philosophy and the Anglophone tradition of analytic philosophy. Following these initial orientations that relate to his personal history, Appiah's persistent focus on individual autonomy stirs additional reflection on how he can be viewed as part of an intellectual tradition influenced by the nineteenth-century British philosopher John Stuart Mill (1806–73), who engaged with the rights and ethics of individual freedom in such treatises as *On Liberty* (1859) and *Utilitarianism* (1863). Appiah's critical engagement with the personal and social repercussions of race in modern society equally places him as an heir to such thinkers as the African-American scholar W. E. B. Du Bois (1868–1963). Appiah has written at length about the ideas and positions of both Mill and Du Bois.

Equally significant is Appiah's generational identity, being part of a post-revolutionary cohort of intellectuals who came of age after pivotal figures of the decolonization era like Fanon, Amílcar Cabral (1924–73), and Kwame Nkrumah (1909–72), Ghana's first president. Though radical activists and intellectuals would continue to emerge in Africa, making this contrast is useful for locating Appiah and rethinking his political concerns. Going further, we should also position Appiah among contemporary thinkers and scholarly trends. The emergence of his work during the late 1980s placed him in discussions of postcolonial studies, with his scholarship on African epistemologies comparable to the interventions of Edward Said (1935–2003) and the Congolese philosopher V. Y. Mudimbe. Finally, Appiah is not alone among present-day academics in his engagement with questions of identity, justice, and cosmopolitanism. An ethical turn has informed literary studies, anthropology, and other fields over the past several decades (Eaglestone 1997; Sanders 2002; Keane 2015; Saint 2018). This book touches upon Appiah's approaches in relation to the contributions of the liberal philosopher John Rawls (1921–2002), the Ghanaian philosopher Kwasi Wiredu, and the American philosopher Martha Nussbaum, among others.

Against this backdrop, there remains a lurking paradox at play. To what extent is it useful, or even appropriate, to identify the intellectual and historical coordinates of a philosopher who himself has frequently eluded and argued against such certainties?

One initial answer is that this book does not pretend to be comprehensive, with attention being primarily drawn to the broad contours of Appiah's thinking. Particular attention is given to how his ideas can be utilized by students and scholars of literature. Furthermore, he is still alive. Appiah is an active scholar, and he undoubtedly will continue to surprise and inform readers with new work. Since 2010 alone, his books have addressed the history of moral revolutions (*The Honor Code*), the education of W. E. B. Du Bois (*Lines of Descent*), the promise and problems of 'idealization' (*As If*), and how recent research in neuroscience and cognitive psychology have contributed to understandings of 'virtue' ethics (decision making based on one's character) versus 'situation' ethics (flexible decision making based on immediate circumstances) (*Experiments in Ethics*). Amid this diversity are certain threads that bind his scholarship as a whole—in particular the roles of moral philosophy and critical reasoning in the making and unmaking of social identities. Ever the philosopher, Appiah habitually positions ethics ahead of politics, in contrast to many of his peers in other academic fields. Ethics for Appiah *is* the starting point of politics.

Along this line, it is important to stress that his scholarship has not escaped debate. As cited earlier, his criticism of group identities has placed him outside a current political mood that has been defined by a range of identity-based social justice movements, whether Black Lives Matter, Rhodes Must Fall, or the #MeToo movement. These campaigns have provided community and solidarity that have offered spaces of safety and power. Furthermore, Appiah's embrace of political liberalism contrasts with the recent vitality of democratic socialism and other leftist politics that have promoted a more radical approach for confronting present-day economic, racial, and gender inequalities. These approaches view these social problems as not a matter of personal ethics or individual choice but as systemic in scope, requiring broader social and political change. The Black Radical Tradition, involving such thinkers as Cedric Robinson, Keeanga-Yamahtta Taylor, and Charles W. Mills, is exemplary of this critique (Robinson 1983; Mills 1997; Taylor 2016; Mills 2017). On the other hand, Appiah's promotion of cosmopolitanism can be received as a provisional antidote to the nativism and right-wing nationalism that has cropped up in the United States, Europe, and elsewhere. His belief in individual choice leading to social change suggests that personal behavior can have wider and long-lasting implications—ethics, once more, as the starting point for politics. Though Appiah may be seen as out of step with some audiences, his philosophy is not without political implications.

This book takes stock of these issues in the chapters that follow—at once situating, explaining, and at times critiquing the dimensions of Appiah's thinking. For the most part, this book moves chronologically, addressing Appiah's work in order of publication to track the evolution of his thought. Furthermore, while providing an overview of his scholarship, it nonetheless emphasizes some books and positions over others. This critical introduction argues that his early study *In My Father's House* set the stage for issues and debates that have brought him to prominence and with which he has continued to grapple. As philosopher Tsenay Serequeberhan has noted, Appiah's book itself exemplifies the original source for the title by containing 'many mansions' (Serequeberhan 1996: 110). I additionally believe it provides the origins for much of his later work. Though categorizing an intellectual like Appiah always carries certain risks, this book positions him as an African philosopher, not only due to his status as a harbinger of recent trends in African writing, but also because the African elements of his interventions—whether Asante customary norms, his father's political career, or his own recollections of growing up in Ghana—provide unique signatures that distinguish his arguments.

Yet, this introduction to Kwame Anthony Appiah will wander a bit, too, with explorations of other thinkers, intellectual trends, historical events, and novels to illustrate his ideas. To borrow a scenario that Appiah himself uses in the introduction to *Thinking It Through*, this book is similar to walking through a foreign city, with streets and byways that can only become intelligible through detours, vantage points, pauses for rest, and the occasional cul-de-sac. 'The trouble is that just when you think you have found your way out of one maze of alleys, you are plunged into another', Appiah writes. 'If, in your wanderings, you climb to the top of a tall tower, you can look down over the streets you have been lost in, and suddenly everything begins to make sense' (TT: xii).

This book provides this kind of architecture to navigate and gain perspective. Though many of the topics raised can only be fleetingly touched upon, it is designed to introduce students of literature and other readers to one of the most significant moral philosophers of our time and why the question of identity is the wellspring of his thought. As he writes in the introduction to *The Lies that Bind*,

> I've set myself the task in this book of discussing some of the ideas that have shaped the modern rise of identity and trying to see some of the mistakes we regularly make about identities more clearly. Philosophers contribute to public discussions of moral and political life, I believe, not by telling you what to think but by providing an assortment of concepts and theories you can use to decide what to think for yourself. I will make lots of claims; but however forceful my language, remember always that they are offered up for your consideration, in the light of your own knowledge and experience. I'm hoping to start conversations, not to end them.
>
> (LTB: xiii)

This book embraces a similar approach. Kwame Anthony Appiah is ultimately a philosopher whose moral imagination is concerned with individual freedom and the ways in which this freedom is abetted or limited by identity. He remains a committed thinker who continues to engage with matters of public importance, whether issues of race or nationalism, whether through media like the BBC or the pages of *The New York Times*. Appiah has been consistently responsive to his time. What more could one want from a philosopher active today?

KEY IDEAS

1

AFRICAN
EPISTEMOLOGIES

In *Thinking It Through*, Kwame Anthony Appiah writes that the study of philosophy often holds a surprise or two for the new student. Rather than raising questions immediately pertinent to the world we inhabit—for example, what is justice?—a philosopher often begins with the question of how to define knowledge itself. What do we know, and how do we know what we know? In Appiah's words, 'a philosopher is likely to start by asking what it is to know anything at all—thus beginning with epistemology, which is the philosophical examination of the nature of knowledge' (TIT: xi).

We can adapt and apply this approach to Appiah himself as an initial step for comprehending his work. What are the personal and historical grounds for positioning Appiah's perspectives? How might these circumstantial, though nonetheless foundational, conditions present a preliminary framework for approaching and explaining his scholarship? This chapter answers these opening questions by arguing that Appiah's Ghanaian background is essential to understanding his worldview. Biography not only provides a context for situating and understanding his oeuvre, but it also allows us to assess the extent to which his experiences can or cannot serve as a basis to generalize about the experiences of other people.

CHILD OF MIDNIGHT, BETWEEN WORLDS

As mentioned in the introduction, to assert one dimension of Appiah's identity over another one is a tricky business, especially for a philosopher who is critical of such moves. As he writes in the introduction to *The Lies that Bind*, random acquaintances often take him for being Indian, Ethiopian, or North African, among other possibilities, due to his racially ambiguous appearance. As he further discusses, the specifics of his family origins do not necessarily make the question of identity clearer. His mother's family has roots in England that can be traced to the thirteenth century. His father's family lineage can be traced to the eighteenth century, in this instance the Asante Kingdom which today is part of Ghana. Complicating matters further are the contrasting kinship practices between the English and the Asante. The former recognizes patrilineal descent while the latter are matrilineal in orientation. In practical terms, Appiah would be expected to align more with his mother's family according to his Ghanaian family, while his British relatives would anticipate a greater sense of belonging with his Asante heritage (LTB: xi, xii).

Though his English background and education are undoubtedly indispensable to his identity, on balance Appiah has engaged with his African birthright more. (Yet, in this very gesture, he may be identifying with a set of English patrilineal norms!) This proclivity is best illustrated in his book *In My Father's House* (1992)—a breakout work that marked a personal turn in his scholarship that contrasts with his previous academic studies. It consists of a series of interventions on a range of topics; it is not seamless and at times betrays an unevenness of focus. Nonetheless, as suggested by the title, which draws from the New Testament passage of John 14:2 ('In my Father's house are many mansions'), the book can be read as a meditation on the world of his father—indeed, the multiple worlds of his father. As Appiah writes in the preface, he inherited from him his African, Ghanaian, Asante, and Christian understandings of the world and the challenges that can attend such identities. Though his mother, Peggy Appiah (née Cripps), was equally a formative influence and intellectual collaborator (Appiah et al. 2007), *In*

My Father's House is dedicated to his father. The conclusion, which ruminates on the dimensions and meanings of his father's funeral, affirms this patrimonial legacy (Nzegwu 1996). By extension, it illuminates in microcosm the experience of being Asante, Ghanaian, Christian, and African all at once and the long history of contradiction and conflict among these identities, which were not unique to Appiah.

Kwame Anthony Akroma-Ampim Kusi Appiah was born on May 8, 1954, approximately three years before the independence of Ghana—formerly the British Gold Coast—in 1957. One could style him as a cousin to one of Salman Rushdie's 'midnight's children' (Rushdie 1981). Like Saleem Sinai, Rushdie's main character, Appiah is part of an inaugural postcolonial generation, born during a 'midnight' period of political transition that portended a new political and historical dawn. Though generations are rarely discreet due to connections and entanglements with preceding and succeeding generations, the notion of 'generation' provides a useful device to frame Appiah and the world he was born into, which had to navigate the effects and meanings of both colonialism and anti-colonialism. His father, Joseph Emmanuel Appiah (1918–90), better known as Joe Appiah, joined the Gold Coast's independence struggle led by the charismatic Pan-Africanist Kwame Nkrumah and the Convention People's Party (CPP). Nkrumah and the senior Appiah became close friends and colleagues for a time during the 1950s. This personal connection and the politics of this period lay the groundwork for Anthony Appiah's engagement with race, Pan-Africanism, and the challenges of African identity more generally.

KWAME NKRUMAH (1909–72)

Kwame Nkrumah was Ghana's first president and an important figure in postcolonial Africa. Of Akan ethnic background and an only child, Nkrumah was educated at mission schools in the British Gold Coast and eventually trained as a teacher. He traveled to the United States in 1935 to study at Lincoln University, a historically Black institution of higher learning in Pennsylvania. He later enrolled at the University of Pennsylvania and spent time in Harlem, where his ideas about Pan-Africanism gestated. His political stature rose when he co-organized the Fifth Pan-African Congress in Manchester in October 1945 with the Trinidadian intellectual George Padmore (1902–59). Nkrumah returned to the Gold Coast in 1947 where he became active in the United Gold Coast Convention, also founded in the same year. In June 1949, he helped establish a new party, the Convention People's Party, through which he implemented the Positive Action campaign to put pressure on the British Colonial Office by staging political protests and worker strikes. Though he was arrested for these activities, Nkrumah eventually became the Leader of Government Business for the Gold Coast in 1951 and, after an election in 1956, the first prime minister of Ghana on March 6, 1957. This position later changed to president in 1960 after Ghana became a republic. Nkrumah became known for promoting Pan-Africanism and decolonization in Africa by helping establish the Organisation of African Unity—what is today the African Union—in 1963 as well as being a vocal critic of apartheid in South Africa. He was also a founder of the Non-Aligned Movement in 1961, which articulated a politics of Third Worldism that sought to work against the Cold War pressures and interventions of the United States and the Soviet Union. Nonetheless, Nkrumah was deposed in a coup supported by the US in 1966. He went into exile, residing in Guinea, and later died in 1972 from cancer. He is widely admired in Ghana and Africa today for being one of the continent's most visionary leaders (see Ahlman 2017 for further discussion).

GHANA AND THE POLITICS OF DECOLONIZATION

The life of Joe Appiah impacted the thinking of his son not only because of matters of paternity, but because the senior Appiah was emblematic of his generation—Western-educated, rooted in African custom, and active in anticolonial politics. If Kwame

Anthony Appiah has written about, and himself personifies, a certain global cosmopolitanism in our present, his father equally embodied a type of colonial cosmopolitanism between the Gold Coast and the British metropole, articulating what the sociologist Paul Gilroy has referred to as the Black Atlantic (Gilroy 1993). Indeed, a long-standing tradition of cosmopolitanism had existed in the Gold Coast and West Africa (Brizuela-Garcia 2014). The Atlantic world not only once hosted a trans-hemispheric economy reliant on the slave trade, but in the wake of this system it also produced a Black counterculture of modernity. This 'Black Atlantic' culture challenged white claims to the Enlightenment ideals of freedom and equality. Integral to this counter-modernity is 'double consciousness' on the personal level—a notion first proposed by W. E. B. Du Bois in his classic sociological study *The Souls of Black Folk* (1903). In Du Bois's mind, African Americans had to maintain two kinds of perception simultaneously: a natural sense of self-perception, but also a concurrent perception as to how whites viewed Blacks. This secondary judgment had the effect of diminishing the dignity and humanity of African Americans through anti-Black racism and the threat of white violence.

This book will return to Du Bois and 'double consciousness' in the next chapter. What is important here is how the politics of the Black Atlantic and the condition of 'double consciousness' can be applied to the Appiahs. Father and son both inhabited multiple worlds—Asante, Ghanaian, Atlantic, and British—to differing effect. Joe Appiah had aristocratic origins in the Asante Kingdom. He was also a member of an ethnically diverse, Western-educated class that emerged during the nineteenth century following the end of the transatlantic slave trade and the establishment of Christian mission schools. His father had been a school headmaster and a member of the Methodist Church in Kumasi, the Asante capital. His father also served as Chief Secretary of the Asanteman Council under Nana Prempeh I, the *Asantehene*—the Twi word for 'king'—during the 1930s. In short, Joe Appiah had firm roots within Asante culture and politics, but also belonged to a generation that balanced and interwove African and European influences The concept of being 'Ghanaian' in a national or cultural sense had not yet been established with the colonial Gold Coast riven by a spectrum of ethnic, cultural, racial, and religious identities—a situation that would last into the postcolonial period.

THE ASANTE

The Asante (also spelled 'Ashanti') people are an ethnic group in Ghana located in the south-central 'middle belt' region of the country, north of the Atlantic coastline. The population of the Asante region is approximately 4.78 million (2010 estimate) with Twi being the most commonly spoken language. The Asante Kingdom was established in the 1670s as the result of a lucrative regional trade in slaves, ivory, and gold. The kingdom and its capital, Kumasi, were well-placed geographically between trans-Saharan trade networks and the Atlantic coastal trade. Its political consolidation concurrent with economic growth made the Asante Kingdom an important political power in West Africa—a state that benefited from European commercial interests, including the transatlantic slave trade through its capturing and selling of slaves, though it would face the ire of these same interests, specifically the British, by the nineteenth century. A series of five wars took place between the British and the Asante during this period, starting in 1824. The first Anglo-Asante War (1823–31) was the longest at seven years. The final Anglo-Asante War, known as the War of the Golden Stool (1900), brought the Asante Kingdom under British control. The Asante continued to govern themselves, however, as part of the colonial system of indirect rule, which recognized local leaders and customary law as a means of naturalizing foreign control. Overall, the Asante have a long history of independence, which in turn has imparted a strong sense of cultural pride and an identity that is equal to, and in many cases older than, a range of European and other national identities found elsewhere in the world (for further discussion, see Wilks 1975; McCaskie 2003).

After attending a sequence of elite Methodist schools in the Gold Coast and holding a position with the United Africa Company in Sierra Leone during the Second World War, the senior Appiah went to Britain where he trained as a lawyer. While in the UK, he became involved with the West African Students' Union, which brought him in contact with a number of important figures who would go on to have distinguished careers, including George Padmore (1902–59), Jomo Kenyatta (c. 1897–1978), Hastings Kamuzu Banda (c. 1898–1997), and Kwame Nkrumah (Appiah 1990: 159–60; Matera 2015). He later met Du Bois at the 1945 Pan-African Congress held in Manchester, which was co-organized by Padmore and Nkrumah. Appiah consequently had friendships with many intellectuals and politicians who would later influence the scholarship of his son. Indeed, Nkrumah was to be Appiah's best man for his wedding to Peggy Appiah in 1953, but eventually had to bow out due to his duties as the Leader of Government Business for the Gold Coast, a role he attained in 1951. Padmore served in his stead (Appiah 1990: 214–16; Caine 2010).

Despite a shared political education and agenda that sought the Gold Coast's independence, Joe Appiah fell out with Nkrumah due to what he perceived as corruption surrounding Nkrumah and his political party, the CPP. In his memoir published in 1990, the senior Appiah described his break from Nkrumah in stark moral terms. 'He [Nkrumah] had become a friend in the fullest and truest sense', Appiah writes, 'but when he saw what was wrong and refused to put it right, he ceased to be a moral being and a friend' (Appiah 1990: 243). Appiah joined the Asante-based National Liberation Movement, a rival to the CPP that held a different vision of a future postcolonial Ghana (Allman 1990, 1993). He remained a firm critic of Nkrumah after independence, experiencing periods of imprisonment as a result (Gates 1990: xvi–xvii). Regarding Nkrumah's eventual removal through a coup, the senior Appiah later remarked, 'Nkrumah's inordinate ambition to achieve a name on the world stage was to provide the opportunity for his total destruction' (Appiah 1990: 271).

DECOLONIZATION

Decolonization commonly refers to the process of pursuing self-determination and achieving political independence in former colonial territories located in Africa, Asia, and the Americas. From a historical standpoint, this phenomenon has been an uneven one stretching across several centuries—from the independence of the United States (1783) and Haiti (1804) during the late eighteenth and early nineteenth centuries to more recent examples of 'transition' and 'hand over' as in the cases of South Africa (1994) and Hong Kong (1997), respectively. Decolonization has, therefore, been a near-universal phenomenon in world history, yet it has also evolved beyond its original diplomatic usage to address questions of social justice and cultural sovereignty. In his classic text *The Wretched of the Earth* (1961), Frantz Fanon (1925–61), the famed psychiatrist and political philosopher who participated in the anti-colonial struggle in Algeria, argued that decolonization must address class inequalities: a postcolonial elite must not simply replace a colonial elite. More recently, African intellectuals like Ngũgĩ wa Thiong'o have promoted a return to Indigenous languages and aesthetics in order to resist the enduring effects of colonialism, as argued in his widely influential study *Decolonising the Mind: The Politics of Language in African Literature* (1986). Social movements like #RhodesMustFall in South Africa and Britain have also invoked a rhetoric of 'decolonization' to promote new university curricula and the removal of monuments to imperial figures like Cecil Rhodes (1853–1902). Decolonization therefore continues to surface in new ways, demonstrating an ongoing critical engagement with the persistent and far-reaching legacies of Western imperialism.

The foregoing political connections and intellectual influences that shaped Joe Appiah's life defined an entire political generation that Anthony Appiah would both learn from and work against. This revolutionary generation that promoted anticolonial activism and a range of Pan-Africanisms, while also cultivating new nationalisms across the African continent, defined the meaning of 'decolonization' through a range of strategies that were political, economic, cultural, and philosophical in scope. Indeed, the politicians and thinkers that emerged at this time—Nkrumah, Frantz Fanon, and Amílcar Cabral, to name only a few—have predominated understandings of African political and intellectual life up to the present. A person on the street, whether in Nairobi or London, is more likely to recognize and celebrate the name of Congolese leader Patrice Lumumba (1925–61) than, for example, Ghanaian philosopher Kwasi Wiredu. Yet it is important to recognize that African intellectual history did not begin or end with the pivotal generation that ushered in the postcolonial period. Kwame Anthony Appiah is representative of the next generation that tackled the legacies of anticolonial activism, including questions of nationalism and political accommodation that his father grappled with, in order to reappraise what could be useful for a postcolonial future.

RACE, RACISM, AND THE PREDICAMENTS OF PAN-AFRICANISM

In his first popular work, *In My Father's House*, published in 1992 after a textbook (Appiah 1989) and two academic studies (Appiah 1985, 1986) that drew on his doctoral research concerning the philosophy of language and mind, Appiah sets forth a sequence of critiques against the concepts of race, Pan-Africanism, nativism, and 'Africa' itself. In sum, he positions himself against the formative ideas and revolutionary ideologies of his father's generation. On the surface, this critical approach might be interpreted as an Oedipal gesture or as merely reactionary against a preceding cohort of intellectuals and their arguments. However, Appiah does pay tribute throughout the book to this generation in different ways. Indeed, it is important not to essentialize the preceding generation, given the tensions between Nkrumah and the senior Appiah over issues of ethnicity and nationalism. Kwaku Larbi Korang has documented a longstanding history of intellectual discourse and exchange in Ghana during the nineteenth and twentieth centuries in which local scholars and thinkers repeatedly raised questions of identity during the 'post-encounter' period (Korang 2004). Both Appiahs fall into this deeper tradition. The conclusion of *In My Father's House* with its discussion of kinship and family in the making of one's identity underscores these generational distinctions and entanglements at once.

Looking forward, the recurrent skepticism toward group identities and politics, which can be found throughout Appiah's scholarship up to *The Lies that Bind* (2018), begins with this book. This stance can be attributed in part to his own identity as cited before. But taking the observations of the previous paragraph further, his emphasis on the individual versus group politics also speaks to a new set of ethical questions after revolution or, in this case, decolonization. To sketch an analogy, we can compare the critical outlook of Appiah toward the politics and ideologies of decolonization to the like-minded critical views of European philosophers such as Georg W. F. Hegel (1770– 1831), John Stuart Mill, and Karl Marx—thinkers who were all different from one another, but whose work grappled with the ideas and legacies of the French Revolution (1789–99). It is this post-revolutionary, generational aspect that is significant, even for Hegel who was born before the revolution, but whose most influential arguments came after. Marx and Mill came to very different conclusions about the legacies of revolution, with Appiah embracing Mill as discussed further in Chapter 4. In this instance, this generational framework is useful for complicating the epochal dimensions of 'colonial' and 'postcolonial', which can impart a problematic temporal uniformity (Hall 1996; McClintock 1992; Prakash 1992; Shohat 1992). Appiah's moral philosophy is reflective of a specific political moment and generational timing.

The key question Appiah confronts in *In My Father's House*, which he shared with a number of post-independence intellectuals, is the initial problem of 'Africa' itself. How is 'Africa' to be reimagined and restored in the wake of Western imperialism? This question is a response to the negative imagery of the continent that rationalized colonialism before and after the Berlin Conference (1885–86), which formalized the 'Scramble for Africa'. One exemplary text is *Heart of Darkness* by Joseph

Conrad (1857–1924), first published in 1902. Based on Conrad's own travels up the Congo River in 1890—in what is today the Democratic Republic of Congo—the story involves a mission by a young protagonist, Marlow, to the upper reaches of the river where he attempts to retrieve a European trader named Kurtz, who has 'gone native'. Kurtz dies on the return voyage, with Marlow fabricating a story for Kurtz's fiancée in Europe as to how Kurtz's life ended—a conclusion imparting the idea that the truth of imperialism can never be told.

Beyond the immediate story, Conrad portrays the Congo and by extension Africa as a place of primitiveness, without history or civilization. This imagery drew upon Christian evangelical beliefs of the time—the contrast of 'light' and 'darkness' in the novella echoes Biblical metaphors for 'good' and 'evil'—as well as ideas of scientific knowledge and superstition that emerged with the European Enlightenment (Brantlinger 1988). The stereotype of 'Darkest Africa' can be further seen in the Victorian-era writings of the missionary David Livingstone (1813–73) and the explorer Henry Morton Stanley (1841–1904). Hegel had claimed that Sub-Saharan Africa was 'the land of childhood, removed from the light of self-conscious history and wrapped in the dark mantle of night' (Hegel 1975 [1837]: 174). Conrad's views therefore did not exist in isolation. He represented an age of empire. Against this persistently negative characterization, the Nigerian novelist Chinua Achebe (1930–2013) mounted a strident critique of Conrad in his essay 'An Image of Africa' (1977) by accusing Conrad of being a racist, a claim that ran against prevailing literary opinion. Though defenders of Conrad have pointed to the multilayered quality of *Heart of Darkness* and its implicit criticism of European imperialism as dystopian in nature, Achebe's intervention has endured (Achebe 1977).

In contrast to Achebe, Appiah takes an unconventional approach to the construct of 'Africa'. Though he is certainly critical of imperial perspectives like those of Conrad, he is also concerned with the less conspicuous influence of Eurocentric epistemologies by underscoring how Black intellectuals in the African diaspora have equally 'invented' Africa to suit their needs. In the first chapter of *In My Father's House*, entitled 'The

Invention of Africa', he addresses this issue, beginning with the case of Alexander Crummell (1819–98), a Cambridge-educated, African-American clergyman who went on to help establish the country of Liberia, an experimental colony founded in 1822 for the repatriation of former slaves from the United States. Though from a generation older than Conrad, they both inhabited the same century and world of empire, if from different vantage points.

What is intriguing and troubling for Appiah is Crummell's inauguration of 'Pan-Africanism' as an idea, but also the manner in which Crummell argued for 'a common destiny for the people of Africa' on the basis of race (IMFH: 5). This 'linking of race and Pan-Africanism' has been 'a burdensome legacy' to Appiah's mind, revealing the inheritance of 'conceptual blinders' from European thought toward Africa (IMFH: 5). Though 'race' served as 'a central organizing principle' for the struggle to decolonize the continent, Appiah contends that the European origins of this concept present dilemmas of essentialization, given the multitude of African societies and histories that challenge racial assumptions of uniformity, leading to a central paradox: How 'African' is 'Pan-Africanism' if it depends on a European concept of 'race'? By extension, there is the thorny question of whether the racial underpinnings of Pan-Africanism make it 'racist' (IMFH: 13–14).

To answer these questions, Appiah first points out that notions of difference tied to physical appearance and descent have ancient origins. There is nothing uniquely 'European' or modern about creating taxonomies of people. To address the trickier question as to whether Crummell and Pan-Africanism more generally are 'racist', Appiah resorts to the distinction between 'racism' and 'racialism'. 'Racialism' refers to the idea that there are 'races' in which 'all members of these races share certain traits and tendencies with each other that they do not share with members of any other race' (IMFH: 13). 'Racialism' is not intrinsically 'dangerous' though Appiah is critical of its premise—a point that will be addressed further in the next chapter (IMFH: 13).

'Racialism', however, can turn into 'racism' depending on the circumstances. Appiah makes a subsequent distinction between two kinds of racism: 'extrinsic racism' and 'intrinsic racism'. The first concept is what is commonly understood and accepted as 'racism'—a subjective view that differentiates and judges other races to be of lesser or greater intelligence with attendant moral capacities. 'Extrinsic racism' is therefore social and outward-looking. It is a schema for evaluating other people. The second concept of 'intrinsic racism' is related, though with emphasis placed on intra-group, rather than inter-group, relations. 'Intrinsic racism' is about favoring members of one's own race because they are members of the same group. It is more internally focused, with fictive likeness and group loyalty fore-grounded ahead of difference from others (IMFH: 14–17). As Appiah puts it: 'It is the assimilation of "race feeling" to "family feeling" that makes intrinsic racism seem so much less objectionable than extrinsic' (IMFH: 17).

PAN-AFRICANISM

Pan-Africanism is a political and cultural movement that has promoted the interests and aspirations of people of African descent. Though Pan-Africanism is often considered to be a set of ideas, it has frequently taken organizational and institutional form—the 1963 establishment of the Organisation of African Unity (today the African Union) being one important culmination of Pan-Africanism. The origins of Pan-African thought go back to the nineteenth century, with diasporic Black intellectuals like Alexander Crummell, Edward Wilmot Blyden (1832–1912), and Martin Delany (1812–85) pushing for Black self-determination in different ways as the abolition of slavery took hold. The colonies of Sierra Leone and Liberia, which were intended as places of return for former slaves, in particular, served as sites for articulating and realizing these ambitions. The transatlantic character of these interactions—Crummell was originally from New York, Blyden from the Danish West Indies, and Delany from West Virginia—proved essential in defining the global parameters of Pan-Africanism. Indeed, the twentieth century witnessed a flourishing of Pan-Africanism, starting with the First Pan-African Conference organized by Henry Sylvester-Williams (1869–1911) in London in 1900. A series of Pan-African

Congresses were later held beginning in Paris in 1919—intentionally at the same time as the Versailles Peace Conference with its atmosphere of national self-determination and the founding of the League of Nations. Complementing this sequence of meetings, which involved figures like W. E. B. Du Bois, George Padmore, and Kwame Nkrumah, were parallel movements, including Garveyism and Négritude. The former emerged during the 1910s under the charismatic leadership of its founder, the Jamaican activist-intellectual Marcus Garvey (1887–1940). Garvey advocated Black separatism and a 'Back to Africa' movement through the Universal Negro Improvement Association (UNIA) and its network of local branches, which extended to West Africa and South Africa. Négritude was a francophone literary and cultural movement founded by Léopold Senghor (1906–2001) of Senegal, Aimé Césaire (1913–2008) of Martinique, and Léon Damas (1912–78) of French Guiana during the mid-1930s. Suzanne Césaire (1915–66), Paulette Nardal (1896–1985), and Jeanne ('Jane') Nardal (1902–93), all from Martinique, were also pivotal in establishing the movement. Through poetry and literature, this undertaking examined and promoted a Black humanism that was autonomous from Western cultural influence. Taken together, these combined movements under the umbrella of 'Pan-Africanism' formed a decisive countermeasure and effort against Western racism and political suppression.

With these ideas in hand, Appiah concludes that Crummell was a 'racialist' for believing in the salience of 'race', though he was furthermore an 'intrinsic' racist due to his efforts to bind Black communities into a common movement. Appiah is reluctant to classify him as an 'extrinsic' racist, given the use of this form of external discrimination to inflict harm and violence against other people, rather than build solidarity. Nazi Germany and apartheid South Africa, while relying on 'intrinsic' racism to bind white communities together, are better examples of 'extrinsic' racism mobilized to consolidate power. Still, Appiah sees both forms of racism as morally wrong, though to different degrees and for different reasons (IMFH: 16–19). What is significant in this instance is that Crummell held a reproachful view of African civilization. 'For Crummell inherited not only the received European conception of race', Appiah writes, 'but … the received understanding both of the nature of civilisation and of the African's lack of it' (IMFH: 32). If Conrad and other Europeans held disparaging perspectives toward the African continent, so, too, did Crummell.

Crummell's thinking, born of the progressivism of his time, therefore reveals its limits despite his future-oriented Pan-Africanism. Appiah does mount a defense of Crummell by historicizing why this contradiction would occur. 'It is tremendously important, I think, to insist on how natural Crummell's view was, given his background and education', he writes. 'However much he hoped for Africa, however much he gave it of his life, he could not escape seeing it above all else as heathen and as savage' (IMFH: 32, 33). To elaborate this historical bind further, Appiah quotes an extended passage from Crummell himself:

Africa is the victim of her heterogeneous idolatries. Africa is wasting away beneath the accretions of moral and civil miseries. Darkness covers the land and gross darkness the people. Great social evils universally prevail. Confidence and security are destroyed. Licentiousness abounds everywhere. Moloch rules and reigns throughout the whole continent, and by the ordeal of Sassywood, Fetiches [sic], human sacrifices and devil-worship, is devouring men, women, and little children.

(As quoted in IMFH: 22–3)

This description of 'darkness' and 'devil-worship' echoes the provocative imagery and language of Conrad. Appiah notes that other Pan-African thinkers of the period held similar attitudes. Edward Wilmot Blyden (1832–1912), a journalist and educator originally from St. Thomas in the Danish West Indies (today the US Virgin Islands), spent significant time in both Liberia and Sierra Leone, a British colony founded in 1808 with the same intention of repatriating former slaves. He, too, advocated Black empowerment, though once more with ideas and writing tainted by European racism. Both Crummell and Blyden promoted Christianity over local cultural values and traditions, with Blyden additionally endorsing Islam as an African belief system later in his life. From a political standpoint, they supported a Western form of republicanism, which, favorably or not, contrasted with many African political practices. Ultimately, Appiah is prepared to defend their positive intentions, but he feels obligated to stress their limitations. 'The racial prejudice that the nineteenth century acquired and developed from the Enlightenment did not derive simply from ill-feeling towards Africans', Appiah comments. 'And Crummell's and Blyden's desire to help Africans was no less genuine for their inability to see any virtue in our cultures and traditions' (IMFH: 22).

POSTCOLONIAL DIALOGUES

Extending from his critique of Pan-Africanism, a key purpose of Appiah's project in *In My Father's House* is to challenge existing stereotypes and clichés of 'Africa' held by later Black intellectuals. Appiah is quick to note the differences between this early generation of Pan-African thinkers and those of the twentieth century, such as Du Bois, who, with regard to Africa, 'sought to celebrate and build upon its virtues, not to decry and replace its vices' (IMFH: 24). It is also important to contextualize Appiah's arguments into a broader pattern of critical work undertaken by African intellectuals after decolonization. Wole Soyinka, the Nigerian writer and recipient of the Nobel Prize for Literature in 1986, has tackled the homogenizing of 'Africa' among both Black critics and non-Africans alike. In particular, he has engaged the Négritude movement, both respecting its efforts at 'race-retrieval' in order to rehabilitate a Black 'racial psyche' while also criticizing its supporters for adopting 'the Manichean tradition of European thought' and superimposing it on 'a culture which is most radically anti-Manichean' (Soyinka 1990 [1976]: 126, 127). The South African writer Ezekiel (Es'kia) Mphahlele (1919–2008) made a similar charge in *The African Image* (1962) and elsewhere, criticizing how the movement's poetry romanticized Africa as an uncomplicated place of innocence—certainly a contrast from the reality of apartheid South Africa (Mphahlele 1962; Mphahlele 1967). Though Négritude continues to be an important intellectual tradition (Diagne 2012), these interventions remain significant.

By the same stroke, the Congolese philosopher V. Y. Mudimbe has examined European fabrications of 'Africa' from the ancient period to the present in two studies, *The Invention of Africa* (1988) and *The Idea of Africa* (1994). Mudimbe's interventions closely resemble in purpose and method those of other postcolonial critics, most notably Edward Said and his classic study *Orientalism* (1978). Mudimbe's concept of 'Africanism' is an analog to Said's 'Orientalism' (Mudimbe 1988: ix). The field of postcolonial studies, which emerged during the late 1970s, was a secondary effect and intellectual outcome of decolonization and the rise of Third Worldism after the Second World War. Scholars such as Said, Gayatri Chakravorty Spivak, and Homi K. Bhabha utilized the post-structural theory of thinkers like Michel Foucault (1926–84), Jacques Derrida (1930–2004), and Jean-François Lyotard (1924–98)—in addition to the earlier example and work of Frantz Fanon, Jacques Lacan (1901–81), and Jean-Paul Sartre—to interrogate and 'deconstruct', to use Derrida's term, colonial knowledge that still endured in the present. *Orientalism* exemplifies this approach. Said argued that imperial maneuvers in the Arab world by the French and British depended not solely on military might, but equally on regimes of knowledge that differentiated and diminished Arab and Islamic civilizations from Western European civilization. Said called this discourse of imperial expertise: 'Orientalism'.

What is important about the concept of 'Orientalism' for understanding Appiah's work is how it pointed to a new way of thinking about colonial power. Colonialism was not only about territorial acquisition and resource extraction, as portrayed in *Heart of Darkness*. It was also a struggle over knowledge. Drawing upon Foucault's arguments that political and social power were determined and reinforced through intellectual discourse, Said examined how European comprehension of Islam, ancient Egyptian history, Judeo-Christian belief, and Arab culture more generally produced an 'episteme'—a 'structure of thought'—that defined the colonized as an inferior 'Other' in racial and cultural terms (Foucault 1982 [1969]: 191).

Such understandings and opinions, whether through travelers' accounts, novels, or scientific reports, rationalized foreign rule. Arab-Islamic societies were construed as 'barbaric', being only one step above African societies (Said 1979 [1978]: 150). Spivak and Bhabha would elaborate Said's foundational position by examining how colonial power impacted the psyche of colonized subjects (Bhabha 1994), as well as affecting the colonized in uneven, gendered ways (Spivak 1988). Spivak has been equally critical of the emancipatory limits of Western ideas, Marxism included, leading to her famous declaration, 'The subaltern cannot speak' (Spivak 1988: 308). The field of postcolonial studies has continued with this theoretical eclecticism, stirring debates over technique and meaning, while balanced with a political commitment against past and present forms of imperialism.

The scholarship of Appiah, Soyinka, and Mudimbe has contributed to this broader postcolonial endeavor. Mudimbe is arguably the best example of this African input; Appiah's later chapter echoes the title of his book. Juxtaposing Appiah's work to Mudimbe's and situating it in postcolonial studies are therefore important for grasping the reception of *In My Father's House* and the salience of the debates Appiah entered. His chapter on 'The Postcolonial and the Postmodern', which will be addressed later in this book, is his most focused statement on the possibilities of postcolonial criticism. And yet, Appiah's generational context is as important as his intellectual relationships to postcolonial thinkers. By birth and by history, Appiah *is* postcolonial—he grew up during the nascent postcolonial period, witnessing both the celebratory aspects of political independence and nation-building, but also the uncertainties and complexities of postcolonial politics. For these direct reasons, we can surmise why Appiah has appraised Pan-Africanism both positively and negatively, why Appiah has promoted ethics and moral philosophy ahead of politics, and why Appiah has since moved beyond the immediate concerns of postcolonial critics, but without abandoning his personal roots. The postcolonial has been one intellectual frame for Appiah, as well as a source of personal experience and self-knowledge.

AFRICAN PHILOSOPHIES

Appiah's approach in *In My Father's House* is not merely one of deconstructing past intellectual legacies. He is also concerned with identifying new projects, central among them being a discipline of philosophy for postcolonial Africa. African philosophy is of course a wide-ranging field thematically and geographically, and Appiah's intervention should not be taken as representative of the discipline. He is primarily concerned with the *possibility* of 'African philosophy', given its multiple origins and strands, than he is with summarizing it. In his chapter 'Ethnophilosophy and Its Critics', Appiah begins with an epigraph by the Beninese philosopher Paulin Hountondji, author of *African Philosophy: Myth and Reality* (1976), who defines African philosophy as 'a set of texts, specifically the set of texts written by Africans themselves and described as philosophical by their authors themselves' (IMFH: 85; Hountondji 1996 [1976]: 33). This approach has stirred debate. Does declaring a work as philosophical *make* it philosophy? Is African philosophy by definition a written tradition, despite the importance of oral literature in many African societies? And, finally, can only Africans practice African philosophy? Appiah takes up these questions to different degrees, dissenting with the notion that African philosophy must be written while also expressing caution about a 'unitary explanation' toward what African philosophy is, which can betray 'definitions borrowed from the European philosophical traditions in which contemporary African university philosophers have been trained' (IMFH: 85).

Appiah first interrogates the definition of 'philosophy' by pointing out that every society, whether European or African, has a 'folk philosophy' which provides a set of concepts, norms, and concerns that a philosopher will draw from, whether these issues be 'good' versus 'evil', ideas of justice, or notions of the divine (IMFH: 86–7). He also underscores divisions within Western philosophy on the basis of nation and language, but more broadly between the continental and analytic philosophical traditions. The latter, as a version of natural philosophy, has gravitated toward the sciences while the former has frequently engaged with literature and the arts. In short, there is no homogenous definition or consensus about what 'philosophy' is, even in the Western canon, despite presumptions of cohesiveness and unity. African philosophers have inherited 'two warring Western traditions' (IMFH: 90). This educational endowment raises fundamental questions about the uses of Western philosophy in Africa and, equally, what African experiences can bring to the Western philosophical tradition.

These questions, combined with fellow Ghanaian philosopher Kwasi Wiredu's point that there is a distinction between talking *about* African philosophy and *doing* African philosophy, lead Appiah to one of his trademark techniques—denaturalizing the terminology and categories of analysis at hand. First, he confronts the term 'Africa' itself once more. 'Why should the Zulu, the Azande, the Hausa and the Asante have the same concepts or the same beliefs', Appiah asks, 'about those matters which the concepts are used to think about and discuss?' (IMHF: 91) Second, he similarly cautions against the uses of race and racialism as a possible Pan-African foundation for African philosophy:

> But black [sic] philosophy must be rejected, for its defense depends on the essentially racist presuppositions of the white philosophy whose antithesis it is. Ethnocentrism—which is an unimaginative attitude to one's own culture—is in danger of falling into racism, which is an absurd attitude to the color of someone else's skin.
>
> (IMFH: 92)

Appiah subsequently positions the territory of Africa and African history as sufficient communal grounds for an African philosophy to emerge (see also Janz 2009). And yet he still questions 'philosophy' itself. 'The most that can be said is that what our problems are will determine what methods are appropriate', he observes, 'and perhaps the problems that concern us now are so different from European philosophical problems that we will have to develop a radically different methodology' (IMFH: 92). This conclusion provokes the suggestion that perhaps 'philosophy' itself may not be an appropriate or accurate expression for the intellectual tasks at hand. 'There is, surely, no more reason to suppose that every intellectual activity in the West should have an African twin', Appiah remarks, 'than there is to suppose that we must have African harpsichords or African sonnets' (IMFH: 93).

Against this layered skepticism, Appiah nonetheless ventures forth to consider and rebuild the possibilities of African philosophy. One approach is the genre of 'ethnophilosophy', which he cites as having colonial origins through its 'founding text' *La Philosophie bantoue* (*Bantu Philosophy*) written by Placide Tempels (1906–77), a Belgian missionary, and published in 1945 (IMFH: 94). Despite its European authorship, Appiah appraises this study as significant and influential—if also limited by its overgeneralization of African thought—due to its general enterprise of taking seriously the existence of local African concepts. 'Ethnophilosophy' continues to form an important strand and point of orientation among African philosophers. The identification of Indigenous taxonomies has been essential to African philosophy, enabling an African metaphysics in all its geographic and cultural complexity to be foregrounded, whether through the Yoruba religious system of *Ifá* as practiced in Nigeria (Soyinka 2012) or through the Nguni notion of *ubuntu* ('humaneness') that has gained popularity in post-apartheid South Africa and beyond (Cornell and Muvangua 2012).

But criticism has also been positioned against this approach of restoration and cataloging. Wiredu and Cameroonian philosopher Marcien Towa (1931–2014) have both argued that the recovery and collection of precolonial traditions serve little purpose if they are unable to address present-day issues. Traditional knowledge endures, but it must meet contemporary needs. Paulin Hountondji, like Appiah, has separately critiqued the 'unanimism'—that is, a conviction in a common set of concepts shared across African societies—that informs many understandings of ethnophilosophy (IMFH: 95). A challenge closer to Appiah's own lifelong preoccupations is the continued problem of comparison with Western philosophy, which Appiah says is unavoidable, but that the uncritical application of Western ideas and methods to African conditions and intellectual frameworks must also be resisted (IMFH: 98). Mudimbe's idea of 'gnosis' with its combination of knowledge, uncertainty, and belief, offers one provisional remedy for negotiating these tensions and debates, albeit through a concept drawn from the Judeo-Christian tradition (Mudimbe 1988).

In summary, Appiah identifies a middle ground, believing in the importance of African epistemologies that are useful in the present and in convivial dialogue with other world philosophies. Only through such tension and interaction can African philosophy as a critical discourse emerge. 'Ethnophilosophy, then, strikes me as a useful beginning', he writes, 'a point from which to strike out in the direction of negotiating the conceptual lives ... of contemporary Africans' (IMFH: 100). He agrees with Wiredu in the endurance and salience of precolonial traditions, but they must contribute positively to modern ideals and society. Appiah cites Wiredu as deploring hierarchies, gendered and otherwise, that can exist within 'traditional society' and its norms, while modern Western science has proven concepts that must be accepted (IMFH: 104). Ultimately, local epistemologies must play a vital role in the postcolonial project of African philosophy. But they must assist in active ways to presentist issues, not merely comprise a form of nostalgia, a museum of past ideas. As Appiah concludes, 'Going beyond the descriptive project of ethnophilosophy is the real challenge of philosophers engaged with the problems of contemporary Africa ... I aspire to a more truly critical discourse' (IMFH: 106).

CONCLUSIONS

Appiah and his work must be situated in terms of geography, history, and generation in order to grasp his motivations and identity as a philosopher. In *Giving an Account of Oneself* (2005), Judith Butler has written that 'critique ... cannot go forward without a consideration of how the deliberating subject comes into being and how a deliberating subject might actually live or appropriate a set of norms' (Butler 2005: 8). With this credo in mind, this chapter has specifically framed Appiah as a philosopher born during a pivotal moment of decolonization. As a consequence of this timing and the influence of his father and his participation in Ghana's independence movement, it is useful to see Appiah as confronting the ideas and ideologies that led to that moment and their strengths and limitations for addressing the postcolonial present and future. Appiah is critical toward Western stereotypes of 'Africa' that have lingered since the nineteenth century, but he also deconstructs Pan-Africanism and what he sees as its 'intrinsic racism'—a parallel to the 'extrinsic racism' of colonial perspectives toward Africa. Appiah finds both instances to be morally problematic, given the abstract and flawed reason embedded within them. Nonetheless, his position has been rebuked for neglecting social and material conditions that inform and demand racial solidarity (Henry 1993; Gordon 1995). Furthermore, Appiah himself has been accused of adopting a Eurocentric view toward Africa, despite his claims to the contrary (Okafor 1993).

Appiah's approach is not solely critical, however, but also restorative, constructive, and in search of new methods. The progression of thought within *In My Father's House* questions what it means to be an African philosopher and what it means to be African. The book is an attempt at creating a new pathway to being both—to be the philosopher and African Appiah wants to be, despite any appearance of surface contradictions. Similar to an argument made by Achille Mbembe (2002), Appiah expresses a belief in the possibility of redefining 'African' identity. Furthermore, working against a prevailing set of opinions (Ngũgĩ 1986), he has asserted the 'shallow' cultural impact of colonialism (IMFH: 7). Appiah has promoted the need to seize upon this fact to inaugurate a new set of critical techniques for the present. Building off this point, philosophers like Tsenay Serequeberhan have criticized Appiah for stressing a functionalist approach—African knowledge as contributing to a 'usable identity'—that neglects how this identity is 'not open to our manipulation or control' (Serequeberhan 1996: 116–7). Yet, there is common ground between respecting deeper histories and seeking remedies for the present. 'For if philosophers are to contribute—at the conceptual level—to the solution of Africa's real problems', Appiah writes, 'then they need to begin with a deep understanding of the traditional conceptual worlds the vast majority of their fellow nationals inhabit' (IMFH: 106). His collection of Akan proverbs, co-authored with his mother, Peggy Appiah, and Ivor Agyeman-Duah, exemplifies the possibilities of restoring and cataloging such local conceptual worlds (Appiah et al. 2007). The importance of inherited cultural knowledge and the sources of identity that follow will continue to animate discussion in the rest of this book.

2

RACE

The most debated issue that Kwame Anthony Appiah has addressed in his work has been the subject of 'race'. It is a topic of broad social importance but also one of personal meaning for him. 'I have been writing and ruminating on questions of identity for more than three decades now', he writes in *The Lies that Bind*. 'My theoretical thinking about identity began, actually, with thoughts about race, because I was genuinely puzzled by the different ways in which people in different places responded to my appearance' (LTB: 6). As introduced in the previous chapter, 'racialism' and its auxiliaries 'intrinsic racism' and 'extrinsic racism' form a central theme of *In My Father's House*. It is an unavoidable one. Race and racism are vital aspects in the shaping of African and African-American identities, but they have also informed modern life more generally. This chapter examines Appiah's engagement with 'race'.

DISCIPLINING RACIAL AND ETHNIC STUDIES

Appiah's engagement with race conforms with an academic landscape that emerged in the United States in the wake of the Black civil rights movement. With the African-American literary critic Henry Louis Gates Jr., Appiah has co-edited a number of introductions and critical anthologies of Black writers such as Zora Neale Hurston (1891–1960), Langston Hughes (1902–67), Richard Wright (1908–60), Toni Morrison (1931–2019), and Alice Walker (Appiah and Gates 1993a, 1993b, 1993c, 1993d, 1993e). These studies, in conjunction with different encyclopedias (Gates and Appiah 1999, 2010), sourcebooks (Gates and Appiah 1996), the influential anthology 'Race', Writing, and Difference (1992), and their revival of the Pan-African journal Transition all illustrate the prolific collaboration Gates and Appiah have had in establishing and legitimating the histories, literatures, and cultural lives of Black communities in the US and elsewhere in the face of latent (and not-so-latent) racial discrimination. The so-called 'culture wars' of the 1980s and 1990s, involving critics like Allan Bloom (1930–92) and Harold Bloom (1930–2019) (no relation) and reflecting the conservative politics of Reaganism and Thatcherism at the time, marked a setback for the pedagogical advances made by ethnic studies (Bloom 1987; Bloom 1994). Appiah, Gates, and figures like Stuart Hall (1932–2014) in Britain were crucial interlocutors against this re-entrenchment of an ethnocentrically white cultural curriculum (Gates 1992; Hall 2016).

Yet, it is important to emphasize that Appiah has not promoted African and African-American studies in a simplistic restorative manner. He has wrestled with the issue of 'race' and the ways in which it can reduce the complexity of African and African-American life. Utilizing 'race' as a foundation for knowledge and study suggested a potentially misleading or false ontology for Black existence. If 'race' was first instantiated through pseudoscientific understandings of intrinsic aptitude and difference, how might an academic discipline based on this deceitful premise raise ethical questions of scholarly purpose and meaning? More specifically, how could the field of African and African-American studies thrive without tacitly reproducing a Eurocentric order of knowledge? Could African and African-American studies be based on a set of concepts and understandings that critiqued the Western scientific and humanistic reason that rationalized the enslavement of Africans and the colonization of the African continent? One approach to answering these questions was to understand how preceding Black intellectuals had grappled with them. It is for this reason that Appiah turned to W. E. B. Du Bois to clarify his thinking on these matters.

HENRY LOUIS GATES, JR. (BORN 1950)

Henry Louis ('Skip') Gates is a professor of English Literature and African and African-American studies who has taught at Yale, Cornell, Duke, and Harvard Universities. Originally from West Virginia, he graduated from Yale University (1973) and earned his doctorate at Cambridge University (1979), where he studied with Wole Soyinka. Gates first met Appiah while at Cambridge. The author and editor of numerous books, anthologies, reference materials, and critical editions, Gates is best known for popularizing African-American studies in the United States through documentary films and television series, as well as for his academic work that has sought to recover lost and forgotten Black writers. Drawing upon the Black Arts Movement of the 1960s and the influence of writer-activists such as Amiri Baraka (1934–2014), Gates's first book, *Figures in Black: Words, Signs, and the 'Racial' Self* (1987), asserted the importance of the early African-American writing by Phillis Wheatley (1753–84), Frederick Douglass (1818–95), and Harriet E. Wilson (1825–1900) in the creation of a 'Black Aesthetic' tradition (Gates 1987: xxv, xxvi, 14). This book and later ones, such as *The Signifying Monkey: A Theory of African-American Literary Criticism* (1988), in turn, sought to establish a practice of Black literary criticism to complement this aesthetic tradition. Beyond his academic scholarship, Gates has produced several award-winning documentaries including *Wonders of the African World* (1999) and *The African Americans: Many Rivers to Cross* (2013), which have introduced African and African-American history and culture to a wider audience. He is also known for his popular writing, including his memoir *Colored People* (1994) and *Thirteen Ways of Looking at a Black Man* (1997), which collected his essays from *The New Yorker*. Gates is currently the Alphonse Fletcher University Professor at Harvard, where he also directs the Hutchins Center for African and African-American Research.

W. E. B. DU BOIS AND 'THE
CONSERVATION OF RACES' (1897)

'The American Negro has always felt an intense personal interest in discussions as to the origins and destinies of races', W. E. B. (William Edward Burghardt) Du Bois writes at the beginning of his essay 'The Conservation of Races' (1897), 'primarily because back of most discussions of race with which he is familiar, have lurked certain assumptions as to his natural abilities, as to his political, intellectual and moral status, which he felt were wrong' (Du Bois 1986: 815). This essay was first delivered as a speech at the inaugural meeting of the American Negro Academy. Du Bois was only 29 years old at the time. He had completed his doctorate at Harvard two years earlier in 1895, becoming the first Black man to do so. His speech exhibited a blend of intellectual acuity and budding political ambition. The main thrust of his remarks, located first in a list of seven numbered conclusions, was, 'We believe that the Negro people, as a race, have a contribution to make to civilization and humanity, which no other race can make' (Du Bois 1986: 825).

This early position not only informed the future political and academic work of Du Bois, but it also influenced the activism and scholarship of many in the century that followed. Du Bois was not the first African American to address the issue of race on political and intellectual grounds. However, from a generational perspective, his intervention marked a fundamental break from a preceding cohort of Black activist-intellectuals who had either witnessed or directly experienced the condition of enslavement. Frederick Douglass (1818–95), the most famous African-American abolitionist of the 19th century, was his most significant predecessor. Born into slavery, Douglass escaped at the age of 20 to the north, where he eventually became a minister in the African Methodist Episcopal Zion Church and the publisher of *North Star*, an abolitionist newspaper. He also wrote a classic memoir, *Narrative of the Life of Frederick Douglass, an American Slave* (1845).

Du Bois had little reason to disrespect the vital contributions Douglass had made to African-American life, but he did disagree with the assimilationist position that Douglass fostered in the aftermath of the American Civil War (1861–65). By the same stroke, Du Bois found himself at odds with Booker T. Washington (1856–1915), the most prominent Black intellectual between the older generation of Douglass and the newly emergent generation that Du Bois represented. Washington had gained prominence as the founder of the Tuskegee Institute (today Tuskegee University), a historically Black school in Tuskegee, Alabama. He believed that Black Americans should empower themselves through industrial skills, hard work, and entrepreneurship. Yet Washington also embraced an accommodationist stance with whites, despite the rise of Jim Crow discrimination in the American South and the white terrorism of lynching, both of which would continue into the 20th century. Washington's 'Atlanta Compromise' speech of 1895, given to a predominantly white audience at the Cotton States and International Exposition in Atlanta, Georgia, captured this position of racial accommodation—a stance that Du Bois criticized as too weak in the face of ongoing anti-Black racism and white violence. Du Bois instead founded the Niagara Movement in 1905 and the National Association for the Advancement of Colored People in 1909 as alternatives for Black activists.

Du Bois's argument for Black separatism, not assimilation, and Black advancement, not accommodation, continued to inform his thinking and that of many elsewhere—from the Pan-African Conference (1900) and Pan-African Congresses (beginning in 1919), in which he was involved, to later movements such as the Black Panther Party and the Black Power movement of the 1960s and 1970s. 'The Conservation of Races' started this trajectory. It explains why Appiah gravitated toward this essay in his early writing on race. Appiah's chapter 'Illusions of Race' from *In My Father's House*—a revised version of an earlier essay entitled 'The Uncompleted Argument: Du Bois and the Illusion of Race' (1985)—encompasses this engagement. As Appiah remarks in the opening to this chapter, Du Bois has the distinction of having lived during a period including both the Berlin Conference, which formalized the colonization of Africa, and the independence of Ghana in 1957, which, along with Sudan's independence in 1956, marked the beginning of the end of European control on the African continent (IMFH: 28). As a consequence of this timing, Du Bois became an heir to Alexander Crummell, Edward Wilmot Blyden, and the Pan-Africanism they established during the nineteenth century. 'Not only did Du Bois live long, he wrote much', Appiah remarks, 'if any single person can offer us an insight into the archaeology of Pan-Africanism's idea of race, it is he' (IMFH: 28).

Du Bois provides a working definition of 'race' in 'The Conservation of Races', one that does not rest on 'the final word of science' (Du Bois 1986: 816). At the time, race 'science' was represented by figures like Arthur de Gobineau (1816–82), whose book *An Essay on the Inequality of the Human Races* (*Essai sur l'inégalité des races humaines*, four volumes, 1853–55) promoted the white race—Aryans specifically—over African ('Black') and Asian ('yellow') races (Mudimbe 1988: 107, 119). Furthermore, his book argued for polygenesis, rather than a shared ancestry of humankind (LD: 84). 'What then is race?' Du Bois queried. He immediately offered as an answer:

> It is a vast family of human beings, generally of common blood and language, always of common history, traditions and impulses, who are both voluntarily and involuntarily striving together for the accomplishment of certain more or less vividly conceived ideals of life.
>
> (Du Bois 1986: 817)

Race, in short, was not only about 'blood' descent—a gesture toward scientific reason—but also about socialization ('language', 'traditions') and 'common history'. Furthermore, it was understood as community-oriented and aspirational, the 'striving together' to attain mutually 'conceived ideals of life'. As Du Bois concludes, science was not essential, since the matter of racial difference had been 'clearly defined to the eye of the Historian and Sociologist' (Du Bois 1986: 817). This multilayered approach to defining 'race' is what attracts Appiah to Du Bois's intervention. At stake was not solely the displacement of pseudoscientific understandings of the time, which located people of African descent at the bottom of a hierarchical framework of humankind. Nor was Du Bois concerned with the purely academic question of how to define 'race' as a social category.

The principal aim of his articulation was to unify, to generate a sense of group solidarity that could achieve ideals beneficial to the Black community, whether local, national, or Pan-African in scope, and thus contribute to human progress more generally.

Appiah's response to Du Bois's position is diagnostic in method, similar to his preceding engagements with Crummell and Blyden. More specifically, he undertakes an 'ideational' approach—that is, he is concerned with the idea of race, how Du Bois and others *think* about race (Appiah and Gutmann 1996: 33). Appiah subsequently argues that 'The Conservation of Races' foregrounds a 'sociohistorical' concept of race and, from the standpoint of logic, comprises a dialectical response to preceding arguments of the time—both pseudoscientific claims as well as positions that were assimilationist in orientation, which were designed to 'deprecate and minimize race distinctions' (IMFH: 30; Du Bois 1986: 815). Yet Appiah tussles with the definitional grounds outlined by Du Bois, particularly with the criteria related to science. Appiah sees Du Bois as unable to escape the pseudoscientific reason of his time. Du Bois's invocations of 'common blood' and 'family' indicate to Appiah the limited frame of biological reproduction. Though families can be created by choice, 'it is plain enough that Du Bois cannot have been contemplating this possibility: like all of his contemporaries, he would have taken it for granted that race is a matter of birth' (IMFH: 31). With regard to Du Bois's sociohistorical approach for substantiating racial difference, here, too, Appiah finds himself in disagreement with Du Bois on the basis of logical inconsistency. Appiah contends that 'common history' can only be ascertained *after* a shared identity is recognized. As he puts it, 'sharing a common group history cannot be a *criterion* for being members of the same group, for we would have to be able to identify the group in order to identify *its* history' (IMFH: 32, his emphasis).

With the claims of language and shared 'impulses' also providing unstable definitional attributes—languages can transfer between racial groups, the identification of 'impulses' is *a posteriori* like common history—Appiah pinpoints geography as Du Bois's remaining criterion for eluding scientific reason. Through the latter's listed examples of 'the Slavs of eastern Europe, the Teutons of middle Europe, the English of Great Britain and America', and so forth, Appiah notes Du Bois's 'superaddition of a geographical criterion: your history is, in part, the history of people who lived in the same place' (Du Bois 1986: 817; IMFH: 33). This underlying reliance on historical geography does not undermine Du Bois's broader purpose of positioning African Americans as having a contribution to make as members of the Black 'race'. But it does perpetuate a reasoning based on descent—in this instance, geographic descent—which shares affinities with biological understandings of racial difference. For Appiah, Du Bois in the end neither evades nor undermines the pseudoscientific reasoning about race at the time. It is only after scientific research caught up to Du Bois's anti-hierarchical argument that the fictitious connections between physical attributes and innate mental ability were confirmed—a consensus that started to emerge late in Du Bois's lifetime and continues with ongoing genetic research in the present (IMFH: 34–9).

Against this backdrop, Appiah concludes 'Illusions of Race' by affirming the title's unambiguous contention. 'The truth is that there are no races', he writes, 'there is nothing in the world that can do all we ask race to do for us' (IMFH: 45). The incompletion of Du Bois's argument, as highlighted in the title of Appiah's original 1985 article, is now resolved, with the findings of present-day science enabling an end to racial pseudoscience. Appiah laments how 'race' is still employed as a 'metonym for culture'—what he later refers to as its 'referential' use (Appiah and Gutmann 1996: 33)—resulting in a 'biologizing' of cultural practices, a point that will be returned to in the next chapter (IMFH: 45). More significantly, Appiah admits that the disproof of racial pseudoscience does not in itself end racism. 'The disappearance of a widespread belief in the biological category of the Negro would leave nothing for racists to have an attitude toward', Appiah remarks. 'But it would offer, by itself, no guarantee that Africans would escape from the stigma of centuries' (IMFH: 39).

Du Bois himself continued to grapple with race as a concept, as indicated in the subtitle of his later work *Dusk of Dawn:*

An Essay Toward an Autobiography of a Race Concept (1940). With the advances of scientific thought and the hindsight of almost half a century since 'The Conservation of Races', Du Bois claimed without hesitancy that the 'scientific definition of race is impossible' (Du Bois 1986: 654). Yet, as Appiah has noted, Du Bois continued to work with a sociohistorical concept of race as exemplified in his chapter 'The Concept of Race' in *Dusk of Dawn*. Reflecting on his essay of 1897, Du Bois expressed his unabated attention to the difficulty of definition. 'Since then the concept of race has so changed and presented so much of contradiction', Du Bois remarked, 'that as I face Africa I ask myself: what is it between us that constitutes a tie which I can feel better than I can explain?' (Du Bois 1986: 639) On the basis of this affective connection, he resorted once more to a language of kinship, descent, and geography through terms and descriptions such as 'fatherland', 'my direct ancestors', 'heritage', and 'color and hair' (Du Bois 1986: 639). Yet, he also goes further to argue that 'the physical bond is least' and skin color is but a 'badge' (Du Bois 1986: 640). In Du Bois's view, 'the real essence of this kinship is its social heritage of slavery' and 'the discrimination and insult' that ensued in its wake (Du Bois 1986: 640).

This later argument of Du Bois and his eventual patriation to postcolonial Ghana in 1960, where he would die in 1963 at the age of 95, leads Appiah to the conclusion that, 'If he [Du Bois] escaped ... racism, he never completed the escape from race' (IMFH: 45). This status at the end of his life was a result of ideals meeting reality—an unavoidable conflict between 'the dream of Pan-Africanism and the reality of American racism' (IMFH: 45). For these reasons, Appiah positions Du Bois as both an 'extrinsic' racist—employing race as a means to differentiate people as highlighted in 'The Conservation of Races'—and an 'intrinsic' racist—exemplified by his commitment to Pan-Africanism and his desire to create a transnational Black community. This judgment of Du Bois has met controversy.

On the basis of his own definitions, Appiah's assessment is difficult to disagree with given that the issue of 'race' was at the heart of Du Bois's thinking throughout his adult life. Appiah rightfully construes him as a man of his time. In view of his own multiracial background, it is unsurprising that Appiah would be skeptical of 'race' and its meaning. He intriguingly compares Pan-Africanism to Zionism, both of which expressed the self-determination of socially marginalized groups and emerged during the 19th century when nationalism as a modern political ideology was taking hold. Appiah commends Du Bois's anti-hierarchical, or 'horizontal', reading of race (IMFH: 46). However, he remains critical due to his inconsistencies in defining 'race' itself. Appiah ultimately and unapologetically identifies the limits of Du Bois's thinking in this early assessment from *In My Father's House*, given the paradox that Du Bois 'was unable to escape the [pseudoscientific] notion of race he explicitly rejected' (IMFH: 46). Nonetheless, these last points have precipitated a bitter debate about Appiah's verdict.

THE PROBLEM OF THE COLOR LINE— COUNTERARGUMENTS TO APPIAH

During the decades between 'The Conservation of Races' and *Dusk of Dawn*, Du Bois produced a number of works that examined the vicissitudes of Black identity and the effects of racism. These works include local studies such as *The Philadelphia Negro* (1899), sweeping historical reassessments like *Black Reconstruction in America, 1860–1880* (1935), and Pan-African works exemplified by *The World and Africa* (1947). His most enduring book has been *The Souls of Black Folk* (1903), a collection of interlinked essays whose popular style earned it a wider audience. Writing in a more personal mode and addressing such topics as Booker T. Washington, Alexander Crummell, the Black Church, Black masculinity, Black music, freedom, personal aspiration, and the death of his infant son, Du Bois depicts the *lived* experience of African Americans rather than dwelling on race from a conceptual standpoint. As he puts it at the start of his first chapter, his book is intended to answer 'an unasked question: unasked by some through feelings of delicacy; by others through the difficulty of rightly framing it' (Du Bois 1986: 363). This question is, 'How does it feel to be a problem?' (Du Bois 1986: 363).

The Souls of Black Folk subsequently examines what it means to inhabit a racial category, one that has been construed through negation. Indeed, it contains his most oft-cited line and, despite the committed empiricism of his text, his most significant concept. Regarding the first, Du Bois writes in 'The Forethought' prior to his first chapter that 'the problem of the Twentieth Century is the problem of the color-line' (Du Bois 1986: 359). As Appiah notes in his later book, *Lines of Descent: W. E. B. Du Bois and the Emergence of Identity* (2014), Du Bois first introduced this idea at the Pan-African Conference in London in 1900 (LD: 61). Regarding the second, Du Bois describes how 'the Negro' is 'born with a veil, and gifted with second-sight in this American world' which imparts 'a peculiar sensation, this double-consciousness, this sense of always looking at one's self through the eyes of others, of measuring one's soul by the tape of a world that looks on in amused contempt and pity' (Du Bois 1986: 364). This idea of 'double-consciousness' represented the fracturing of the Black sense of self into a 'two-ness—an American, a Negro; two souls, two thoughts, two unreconciled strivings; two warring ideals in one dark body, whose dogged strength alone keeps it from being torn asunder' (Du Bois 1986: 364–5). While Du Bois's prescient adage about the twentieth century can be grasped immediately, the notion of 'double-consciousness' and its attendant metaphor of 'the Veil', which concealed the 'deeper recesses' of Blackness from the white public, have offered frameworks and tools for deeper rumination about Black identity (Du Bois 1986: 359).

Double consciousness provided a methodological ground for Du Bois's sociohistorical approach to race. Indeed, critics of Appiah's interpretation of 'The Conservation of Races' have stressed the importance of this dimension rather than viewing it as a weak rationale for sustaining the concept of race. It is important to remember that Du Bois's essay was not solely a critique of pseudoscience, which Appiah dwells on, but it was also a critique of racial assimilation. The philosopher Lucius Outlaw has argued that Du Bois was not seeking to eliminate 'race' as claimed by Appiah, but rather wished to articulate race as a '*cluster* concept' that incorporated 'references to biological, cultural, and geographic factors thought characteristic of a population' (his emphasis, Outlaw 1996: 20). Rather than evincing inconsistency, Outlaw sees Du Bois's approach as exhibiting 'his courageous intellectual independence and brilliant creativity' that went against prevailing scientific assessments of race (Outlaw 1996: 26). Furthermore, Outlaw contends that 'race' has generated 'communities of meaning' that are 'highly desirable' for political organization and social relationships beyond the amplitudes of debate over definition (Outlaw 1996: 34; Jeffers 2017). Robert Bernasconi has similarly positioned Du Bois as having already responded to the pseudoscientific race thinking of his time through such works as the sociological study *Race Traits and Tendencies of the American Negro* (1896). Du Bois did not question the entire salience of 'race' as such (Bernasconi 2009). Embracing a broader intellectual context, Robert Gooding-Williams has positioned Du Bois's approach to race in 1897 as impacted by his preceding time in Germany as a student and the academic debates there—a point that will be revisited, given Appiah's own re-examination of Du Bois at that time (Gooding-Williams 2009: 37; Gooding-Williams 1996). Lewis Gordon has been among Appiah's harshest critics, arguing that the inconsistent attributes of 'race' do not make the practice of racism or racist social conditions of inequality any less real, material, or harmful. As he puts it, 'Scientific fiction does not entail social fiction, and semantic fiction does not entail syntactical invalidity' (Gordon 1997: 122).

These critiques in the wake of Appiah's intervention, combined with Du Bois's own writing, not only contrast with Appiah's assessment of Du Bois as a 'race' eliminativist who failed to achieve this aim, but they have also amplified the intellectual and political ambitions of Du Bois's original essay. Indeed, the sociohistorical approach of Du Bois has become commonplace. The idea that race is a 'social formation' that is 'socially constructed', as argued by Michael Omi and Howard Winant in *Racial Formation in the United States* (1986), is now mainstream. While this recent articulation differs from 'The Conservation of Races' by stressing the ways in which 'race' is made and unmade through political, economic, and cultural interactions rather than descent, it nonetheless builds upon Du

Bois's pioneering interpretation. Omi and Winant themselves situate Du Bois among other thinkers of the early 20th century, such as the sociologist Max Weber (1864–1920), the anthropologist Franz Boas (1858–1942), and the Harlem Renaissance poet and intellectual Alain LeRoy Locke (1885–1954), who were all critical of biological understandings of race (Omi and Winant 1994: 65). To offer another example from a different discipline, the African-American philosopher Tommie Shelby has drawn upon the historical 'black strivings' of *The Souls of Black Folk* and the 'badge' of slavery described in *Dusk of Dawn* to establish the moral grounds for present-day movements of Black solidarity against racial injustice (Shelby 2005: 243–4). Du Bois's sociohistorical approach remains influential across fields.

ZORA NEALE HURSTON (1891–1960) AND *THEIR EYES WERE WATCHING GOD* (1937)

Zora Neale Hurston was an African-American writer, anthropologist, and filmmaker. Born in Alabama and raised in Florida, she studied at Howard University and Barnard College, where she received her BA in 1928. She went on to enroll in the graduate program in anthropology at Columbia where she studied with Franz Boas. Hurston also worked with the anthropologist Ruth Benedict (1887–1948), author of *Patterns of Culture* (1934), and had as a fellow student Margaret Mead (1901–78), who would gain prominence following the publication of her groundbreaking study of sexuality, *Coming of Age in Samoa* (1928). During this period in New York, Hurston came into contact with writers of the Harlem Renaissance, including Langston Hughes and Alain Locke. She contributed to the latter's foundational anthology *The New Negro* (1925). A prolific writer of fiction, essays, and ethnography, Hurston's best-known work is the novel *Their Eyes Were Watching God* (1937).

Hurston's novel tells the story of Janie Crawford, a Black woman in Florida who recounts her family history and emotional life to a friend, Pheoby. Crawford depicts a history of generational and gendered violence. Her grandmother, Nanny, was born into slavery and raped by her white owner. Crawford herself was born of sexual violence after her mother, Leafy, was raped by her schoolteacher. The remainder of the novel addresses Crawford's search for emotional stability through three marriages, each of which portrays the different roles Black women were expected to play, whether as a servant, as property, or as a silent and controlled object of beauty and desire. Her third husband, Tea Cake, proves to be the love of her life. However, the novel ends tragically with Crawford killing him in self-defense after he succumbs to rabies and attacks her following a hurricane.

Though received negatively upon first publication, *Their Eyes Were Watching God* has since gained status as a classic work of the Harlem Renaissance period, influencing a number of writers due to its intersectional examination of race and gender and its attention to the vulnerabilities and resilience of Black women. Hurston died in obscurity, with the writer Alice Walker helping restore her to prominence during the 1970s. Hurston's other books include the ethnography *Mules and Men* (1935) and the posthumous works *Every Tongue Got to Confess* (2001) and *Barracoon* (2018).

However, the most sustained engagement with Du Bois's influence and legacy can be witnessed in African-American writing, fiction and non-fiction, during and after his lifetime. The Harlem Renaissance or New Negro Movement—named after Locke's anthology *The New Negro: An Interpretation* (1925)—during the 1920s introduced a generation of Black writers to the American literary scene, including Langston Hughes, Zora Neale Hurston, James Weldon Johnson (1871–1938), and Jean Toomer (1894–1967). Hurston's novel *Their Eyes Were Watching God* (1937), Johnson's memoir *The Autobiography of an Ex-Colored Man* (1927), and Toomer's experimental work *Cane* (1923), in concert with the jazz poetry of Hughes, channeled the complexities of Black life and identity through a range of genres. These and other works responded to, elaborated, and diverged from the observations of *The Souls of Black Folk*, whether the pleasures of music, the mortality of loved ones, the undermining of Black masculinity, or, in the case of Hurston, the emotional lives of Black women. Later novels like *Native Son* (1940) by Richard Wright and *Go Tell It on the Mountain* (1953) by James Baldwin (1924–87) similarly addressed themes of masculinity and Black Christianity identified by Du Bois. *Invisible Man* (1952) by Ralph Ellison (1913–94) can also be read as a reformulation of Du Bois's metaphor of the veil, with African Americans being rendered 'invisible' due to the racism of American society.

The literature of the civil rights generation extended socio-historical understandings of Black identity by becoming more explicitly political in orientation. Baldwin's long-form essays in *The Fire Next Time* (1963) captured the sentiments and outlooks of many African Americans who looked anxiously upon the political possibilities unfolding with the civil rights movement, touching upon issues of race, religion, and masculinity once more. During the same period, the poet Amiri Baraka (LeRoi Jones) published *Blues People: Negro Music in White America* (1963) and *Black Music* (1968), which were works of music criticism that nonetheless underscored, like Du Bois, the soul-making effect music had on Black life. Baraka founded the Black Arts Movement during the 1960s as a cultural counterpart to the civil rights struggle. A newer cohort of writers was also emerging, with their writing reflecting direct involvement in the civil rights movement. *The Autobiography of Malcolm X* (1964), co-authored by X (Malcolm Little) (1925–65) and Alex Haley (1921–92), who would later publish *Roots* (1976), is a classic memoir of a radical civil rights leader's turn to politics. The prison memoir *Soul on Ice* (1968) by Eldridge Cleaver (1935–98) and the epistolary account *Soledad Brother* (1970) by George Jackson (1941–71) captured the experience of incarceration. Angela Davis, who was also imprisoned for her activism, published an autobiography in 1974 and later a study of Black feminism, *Women, Race & Class* (1981)—a work that can be juxtaposed to the critical writing of bell hooks and Audre Lorde (1934–92) (hooks 1981; Lorde 1984; see also Spillers 2003). Not least is the fiction of Toni Morrison (1931–2019), who would become the first African-American writer to receive the Nobel Prize in Literature in 1993.

This sketch of African-American writing since 'The Conservation of Races' demonstrates the ways in which Du Bois's sociohistorical understanding of race continued to flourish. *The Souls of Black Folk* remains a touchstone for Black identity in the US with themes that continue to resonate. This overview is not intended to portray Appiah as against historicism or as naïve about the ongoing significance of race and its formations in African-American life. Appiah's editorial work cited earlier highlights his commitment to elevating African-American literature and culture. However, it must be stressed that Appiah's argument against the racialism of Du Bois is dedicated to a particular logic. Appiah does not fault Du Bois for emphasizing the Black experience, or for believing that African Americans can contribute to American society and the world at large. Rather, his contention is that Du Bois does not completely escape the ideational reasoning of racial pseudoscience and its logic of descent. For Appiah, this predicament speaks to the fraught entanglements of race and the persistent difficulty of escaping the clutches of 'racialism', even today.

TONI MORRISON (1931–2019) AND
THE BLUEST EYE (1970)

Toni Morrison (born Chloe Ardelia Wofford) was the first African-American writer to receive the Nobel Prize in Literature. She published 11 novels, in addition to children's literature and criticism. Born in Ohio, she studied at Howard and Cornell University, where she completed a master's degree on Virginia Woolf and William Faulkner. After holding several teaching positions, including spending seven years at Howard, she became an editor at Random House, where she played a vital role in publishing and nurturing the careers of many Black authors, including Gayl Jones and Angela Davis. Morrison also began her writing career in earnest. Her best-known novels include *Song of Solomon* (1977), which received the National Book Critics Circle Award, and her most acclaimed work, *Beloved* (1987), which won the Pulitzer Prize.

The Bluest Eye is Morrison's first novel, and it foreshadows many of the themes that would preoccupy her fiction in the decades ahead, including intergenerational conflict, gender violence, the responsibilities and betrayals of kin, and, not least, the tragic effects a racist society can have on the behavior and psyche of individuals. Similar to Hurston, Morrison is concerned with the emotional lives of women, thus counterbalancing the views and influence of writers like Du Bois, Wright, and Ellison, while at the same time, like these writers, giving life and meaning to what resides behind 'the Veil'. The Bluest Eye illustrates this sense of purpose through its main protagonist, Pecola Breedlove, who believes that if she had blue eyes—a white form of beauty—her life would be better. Her childhood in Ohio is one of instability and violence, with her parents struggling and her father, Cholly, raping her twice, resulting in pregnancy and a child that dies prematurely. This course of events leaves Pecola psychologically broken. Using multiple perspectives to tell her story, including those of another child, Claudia MacTeer, Morrison underscores the racial limits of opportunity and amelioration in American society and the effects such constraints have on the most vulnerable—in this instance, a young Black girl.

THINKING BEYOND THE COLOR LINE—COMPARISONS TO APPIAH

Appiah was not alone in his larger ambition of eliminating 'race'. Among the most prominent interventions during the same period is Paul Gilroy's *Between Camps: Nations, Cultures and the Allure of Race* (2000b), which was published with the pithier title *Against Race: Imagining Political Culture Beyond the Color Line* (2000a) in the US. This work succeeded *The Black Atlantic: Modernity and Double Consciousness* (1993)—a text that restored and refurbished the Pan-African project for the uses of critical social theory, as touched upon in the previous chapter. Rich with ideas, the central argument of the book is that the transatlantic slave trade not only contributed to economic growth and the industrialization of Western Europe and the Americas, as examined by Eric Williams, Sidney Mintz, and Joseph Inikori, but the history of enslavement in the Atlantic world generated an alternative modernity counterposed to the hegemonic European one (Williams 1994 [1944]; Mintz 1985; Inikori 2002). Furthermore, the technique of using the Atlantic world as a framework intended to disrupt the limited purview of local ethnic identities and racial nationalisms from both analytic and political standpoints. As Gilroy writes,

> In opposition to both of these nationalist or ethnically absolute approaches, I want to develop the suggestion that cultural historians could take the Atlantic as one single, complex unit of analysis in their discussions of the modern world and use it to produce an explicitly transnational and intercultural perspective.
>
> (Gilroy 1993: 15)

Like Appiah, Gilroy has roots in Britain. His father was English, and his mother was the noted Guyanese writer Beryl Gilroy (1924–2001), a member of the Windrush generation—the term 'Windrush' referring to the name of the ship that brought one of the first groups of immigrants to Britain. Gilroy is also a former student of Stuart Hall (1932–2014), the acclaimed social theorist, activist, and cofounder of *New Left Review*. As director of the Centre for Contemporary Cultural Studies at the University of Birmingham, Hall was a pivotal figure in establishing cultural studies as a field both in Britain and internationally. His embrace of the Marxist thinker Antonio Gramsci (1891–1937), in particular, and his subsequent writing on issues of cultural hegemony became widely influential, introducing ways of thinking about race, class, nation, and culture together. Hall's impact is evident in Gilroy's first book, *There Ain't No Black in the Union Jack* (1987), a study of race and class in Britain. But, as the subheading of *The Black Atlantic* indicates, Gilroy's work is also deeply influenced by Du Bois and the concept of 'double consciousness', which he extends beyond the context of the US to understand the experience of 'race' in other social and cultural contexts. In Chapter 4 of *The Black Atlantic*, Gilroy discusses the transatlantic movements of Du Bois to demonstrate this possibility and the international foundations of his thinking.

'Du Bois is also appealing and important from the point of view of this book because of his lack of roots and the proliferation of routes in his long nomadic life', Gilroy writes (Gilroy 1993: 117). These excursions to Germany, Britain, and eventually Ghana with their elements of study, displacement, return, and relocation played key roles in the evolution of Du Bois's ideas, both situating and de-provincializing them at once.

Between Camps extends Gilroy's engagement with Du Bois. It comprises a project similar in ambition to the one embedded in *In My Father's House*. Both Appiah and Gilroy seek to deconstruct the import and legacies of 'race' at the end of the 20th century. The millennial timing of *Between Camps* appears intentional. 'The modern times that W. E. B. Du Bois once identified as the century of the color line have now passed', Gilroy begins his book. 'Racial hierarchy is still with us' (Gilroy 2000b: 1). In contrast to Appiah, Gilroy is not concerned with matters of definition and the pervasive influence of pseudo-scientific reason. Rather, he expresses concern over the racial legacies of European fascism and their continued effect on contemporary nationalist movements. For Gilroy, the uncompleted argument of dissolving the detrimental effects of the color line is therefore not rescued by advances in genetic research as with Appiah, but can only be concluded by grasping the reproduction of malignant forms of biopower through the mutually constitutive categories of 'race' and 'nation'. Identifying continuities between the past and present is essential. Drawing on the work of the French historian-philosopher Michel Foucault, Gilroy believes that the rise of modern authoritarian biopolitics, with its concern for managing populations, and the rise and persistence of 'race', even after the falsification of eugenic thought, is no coincidence (Foucault 1990 [1978]; Foucault 2008 [2004]). As he writes,

> what place should the history and memory of past conflicts with fascism have in forging the minimal ethical principles on which a meaningful multiculturalism might be based? Answering that question takes us into an initial confrontation with the idea of "race" and the raciological theories to which it has given rise.
>
> (Gilroy 2000b: 5–6)

With this observation in mind, Gilroy proposes that 'the old, modern idea of "race" can have no ethically defensible place' (Gilroy 2000b: 6).

The agenda against race in Gilroy's work is far more sweeping than that found in Appiah's engagement with Du Bois, which is centered solely on the issue of race science from a single essay and a Hegelian dialectical logic that depends on establishing an 'antithesis' to the 'thesis' of race (IMFH: 30). Gilroy's approach is sociohistorical in nature and, in this sense, he has no argument with Du Bois's definitional move from science to social and historical empiricism. Rather, he seeks to move beyond the claim that the 'pursuit of liberation from "race"' is a straightforward matter of escaping 'an inferior position in the enduring hierarchies that raciology creates' (Gilroy 2000b: 15). Gilroy wants an end to 'race' entirely and the biopolitical structures it has sustained. As figures like Frantz Fanon and Martin Luther King Jr. (1929–68) have highlighted, in different ways, race-thinking dehumanizes the racist perpetrator in addition to the victim of racism. Indeed, in a foreword to *Black Skin, White Masks* (2008 [1952]), Appiah cites Fanon as critical of anti-Black racism by whites, while also calling for, in Fanon's words, 'a genuine communication' that enables a mutual departure from 'the inhuman voices … of their respective ancestors' (Appiah 2008: x). Though it is impossible to summarize Gilroy's project conclusively in the space allotted here, he finishes his book by looking to a future that embraces a 'planetary humanism' through a tactic of 'strategic universalism' in order to undermine and displace the race-thinking of the preceding centuries.

As with Appiah, Gilroy's positions have provoked debate. Of note, specifically, is his suggestion of similarities between European fascism and what he refers to at one point as 'the authoritarian and proto-fascist formations of twentieth-century black [*sic*] political culture' (Gilroy 2000b: 333). In Gilroy's purview, Black movements have echoed fascist maneuvers, at times, by indulging racial romanticism and glorifying past achievement as a step toward achieving a new era of greatness. The title term 'camp' and its more active form 'encampment' are used by Gilroy to signal the territorial aspirations and needs of nations and nation-states. But he also invokes the term to describe the emergence of 'camp mentalities' that appeal to national and ethnic purity through notions of blood and race (Gilroy 2000b: 82–3). More menacingly, this terminology possesses a distinct dimension of militarism, with camps being a 'political technology' that has resulted in violence and genocide in Europe and its colonies. The 'camp' has enabled forms of 'catastrophic modernity' (Gilroy 2000b: 85–6). To be 'between camps' is therefore to occupy a position of critical distance. It can be 'a positive orientation against the patterns of authority, government, and conflict that characterize modernity's geometry of power' (Gilroy 2000b: 84). Recalling his past work, Gilroy cites a diasporic framework as further means for thinking through and inhabiting this critical liminality. Nonetheless, like Appiah, Gilroy's intervention has stirred reflection on whether 'race' can be discarded and to what end. Though 'racism' remains a social affliction, racial identity as wrestled with by Du Bois can also be a source of empowerment through community and history.

RACE IN THE 21ST CENTURY

With the election of Barack Obama as president of the United States in November 2008, commentators of various backgrounds began to ask if the US had entered a 'post-racial' era, with the racial divisions of the past finally transcended. Less than five years later, in July 2013, the Black Lives Matter (BLM) movement was founded in the wake of the death of Trayvon Martin (1995–2012) and the legal acquittal of his murderer. Since 2013, there have been a number of cases involving the killing of unarmed African Americans by police—most recently George Floyd (1973–2020) and Breonna Taylor (1993–2020) at the time of the writing of this book—that have given further momentum to BLM and its social justice agenda. 'We are unapologetically Black in our positioning', states the BLM's website in terms of its beliefs and principles. 'In affirming that Black Lives Matter, we need not qualify our position' (https://blacklivesmatter.com/what-we-believe/). Globalism, empathy, diversity, gender equality, queer affirmation, and intergenerational solidarity are also part of BLM's program, though the centrality of Black identity remains.

If race appears to be an issue that will not go away, it can partly be attributed to the endurance of sociohistorical legacies identified by Du Bois. The color line continues. The interventions of Appiah and Gilroy must also be situated historically, reflecting, if not always in direct or comprehensive fashion, the problem of apartheid South Africa (for Appiah) and the opportunities of the post-apartheid period (for Gilroy) after the election of Nelson Mandela (1918–2013) in 1994 (Gilroy 2005). Writing in the late apartheid period, Appiah confronted apartheid as a blatant case of 'extrinsic racism' in contrast to the 'intrinsic racism' of Alexander Crummell's Pan-Africanism (IMFH: 16–17). This distinction is important, and yet, similar to Gilroy, the race-thinking of both cases is what troubled Appiah. Writing in the early post-apartheid period, Gilroy suggested that

> if the status of "race" can be transformed even in South Africa, the one place on earth where its salience for politics and government could not be denied, the one location where state-sponsored racial identities were openly and positively conducted into the core of a modern civic culture and social relations, then surely it could be changed anywhere.
>
> (Gilroy 2000b: 27)

These two moments in the 1990s and 2000s, which signaled the idea of racial difference in decline, appear optimistic in retrospect, with debate still continuing among scholars about how to approach 'race' and its meanings for the 21st century. Historians Barbara Fields and Karen Fields have positioned 'race' as a myth, but 'racism' as a fact. Drawing from Appiah, they discuss how 'racecraft', like witchcraft, constitutes a form of unreason that nonetheless has a social impact (Fields and Fields 2012). Akin to Du Bois's position against minimizing racial differences, Ibram Kendi has made a parallel argument that the only way to confront racism—to be anti-racist—is to acknowledge the fact of 'race' and its systemic embeddedness in social structures and political policies (Kendi 2019). In a separate vein, Saidiya Hartman, Christina Sharpe, and Fred Moten have further revised Du Bois's socio-historicism to articulate the dimensions of a Black ontology, which, in Sharpe's words, reflects 'our abjection from the realm of the human' (Sharpe 2016: 14; Hartman 1997; Moten 2017). This Black being and the anti-Blackness that shapes it are not easily dispensed with, but foundational to existing definitions of the human.

These dynamic interventions underscore the recurrence and evolution of thinking on 'race' and how abolishing 'race' as such is not an aim for some scholars, but redefining it as a source of empowerment is. The anthropologist John L. Jackson has stressed the ongoing difficulty of ending race and racism—their zombie-like nature—despite the insights and contributions of many. Race continues to 'haunt' the present. 'No, race is not alive, not anymore', he writes. 'We've killed it, deconstructed it to death, social-constructionized it out of fully animate existence. But it is hardly that easy. Instead, our beast has risen from the dead and haunts our every waking hour' (Jackson 2005a: 400; see also Jackson 2005b). As he further puts it, both seriously and with a dose of humor, 'we need new incantations, new charms and southern amulets, new spells for countering the powerful magics of pseudoscience and social constructionism' (Jackson 2005a: 401). Drawing upon the work and legacy of W. E. B. Du Bois, Appiah has contributed to this broad endeavor of understanding the persistence of 'race' by outlining an ethical stance in contrast to Du Bois's political one. Appiah has also notably revised his views on Du Bois, which will be discussed in the next chapter. Race and the ways it might be utilized, or ended, for future generations remains a significant theme in Appiah's scholarship.

3

CULTURE

If 'race' provides an unstable source of identity, might 'culture' provide a more secure foundation? 'It hasn't escaped notice that "culture"—the word—has been getting a hefty workout in recent years', Appiah remarks in *The Ethics of Identity* (EI: 114). He focuses on how 'culture' and 'diversity' have become entangled with 'cultural diversity' signaling a social and political aspiration for many, but with a lack of clarity as to how these two terms and their combination are to be defined. Appiah notes the paradoxes of 'diversity' in countries such as the United States, where diversity is held as an ideal, but where there are also strong trends of conformity in terms of language, religious belief, and so forth. 'You might wonder', Appiah comments sardonically, 'whether there isn't a connection between the thinning of the cultural content of identities and the rising stridency of their claims' (EI: 117). This chapter examines how 'culture' adds another key dimension of Appiah's interrogation of 'identity'.

'RACE' AND 'CULTURE' COMPARED

'Culture' has often served as an alternative to 'race'. Indeed, 'culture' is frequently counter-posed to 'race'. The German-born anthropologist Franz Boas, who promoted an anti-racist stance through cultural understanding, contended that there was no 'direct relation between race and culture' in terms of heredity. 'The error of the modern theories is due largely to a faulty extension of the concept of individual heredity to that of racial heredity', he writes in the essay 'Some Problems of Methodology in the Social Sciences' (1930) (Boas 1982: 265). Boas agrees that hereditary characteristics *can* have social effects and cultural value—skin color, for example, can result in racism and community solidarity alike—but, as he summarizes, 'Any attempt to explain cultural forms on a purely biological basis is doomed to failure' (Boas 1982: 265).

This critical position has left scholars to grapple with the truth of 'culture'. To cite one academic tradition, the anthropologist Clifford Geertz (1926–2006) made the influential argument that 'culture' is a matter of interpretation. There is no objective 'culture'. In his words, 'culture as a natural fact and … culture as a theoretical entity tends to get blurred' (Geertz 1973: 15). The historical anthropologist James Clifford has worked in a similar vein to argue against 'any transcendent regime of authenticity', with cultural identity always being 'mixed, relational, and inventive' (Clifford 1988: 10). Meanwhile, to draw from another academic lineage, the cultural studies theorist Stuart Hall has stressed the tensions within 'cultural identity'. On the one hand, 'cultural identity' provides a sense of solidarity and 'oneness' based on 'common historical experiences and shared cultural codes' (Hall 1990: 223). On the other hand, 'cultural identity' is also about 'difference', with 'ruptures and discontinuities' making identity an act of tentative 'becoming' rather than solely 'being'. In Hall's words, identity in these circumstances 'belongs to the future as much as to the past', thus working against any understanding of descent-based 'primordialism' (Hall 1990: 225).

Taking these observations further, it is important to underscore how 'culture' has been used to assist statist projects of political exclusion. Colonial rule in Africa and Asia frequently involved the mobilization of cultural difference as a means of divide-and-rule (Mamdani 1996; Cohn 1996). Control was rationalized by employing local authorities and customary law as a means of making colonial rule appear normal. The patina of respect for cultural differences took its most malignant form under the apartheid regime (1948–94) in South Africa, which justified its system of ethnic 'homelands' and white minority rule on the basis of cultural difference. The combined efforts of figures like Nelson Mandela, who was part of the leadership of the African National Congress, and Steve Biko (1946–77), who helped establish the Black Consciousness Movement during the 1970s, dispelled this misleading rationalization by highlighting the systemic racism in place and by promoting forms of multiracial alliance and Black nationalism, respectively—a case when racial solidarities proved vital *against* cultural divisions (Mandela 1994; Biko 1978).

Appiah's engagement with culture can be set against this backdrop. It occurred at a time when many scholars addressed the 'cultural turn', which renewed attention to 'culture' as a specific and elusive category of analysis (Hunt 1989; Jameson 1998). As discussed in the previous chapter, Appiah is critical of race as a form of identification, given its origins in pseudoscience. He is more sympathetic to culture as a source of identity as noted in Chapter 1, though he has expressed skepticism about its uses over the course of his career, most recently in *The Lies that Bind* (2018). In that book, Appiah scrutinizes the matter of culture in one instance through the ordinary examples of 'Western civilization' or 'the West' as shorthand—expressions whose meanings have shifted over time to signal a Greco-Roman heritage, Christian faith, liberal democracy against Soviet communism, and a geography counterposed to the 'non-Western' world. The expression 'Western civilization' demonstrates how cultural terminology can be situational and imprecise, imparting more fiction than fact and leaving an unstable ground for identity claims. 'This way of speaking takes notice of the whole world, but lumps a whole lot of extremely different societies together', Appiah elaborates, while 'at the same time, it delicately carves around nonindigenous Australians and New Zealanders and South Africans, so that "Western" here can look simply like a euphemism for white' (LTB: 191).

Race and culture, then, can be hard to disentangle. The psychiatrist and philosopher Frantz Fanon, whom Appiah has engaged as cited in the previous chapter, is among the most well-known critics of this overlap. His first book, *Black Skin, White Masks* (1952), is a polemic against French racism and cultural chauvinism—how it was impossible for him, as a Black man, to be considered French, despite his French citizenship at birth, his elite education in France, his military service in the Free French forces during the Second World War, and his fluency in the French language. As Fanon recalls in his chapter 'The Lived Experience of the Black Man' (also translated as 'The Fact of Blackness'), the crying of a racist epithet directed at him by a white child symbolized this predicament. It was accepted, even among children, that Black men and women were inferior. In other chapters, Fanon examines the limits of assimilation through language and interracial relationships. He writes in a manner both professional and personal, reflecting his training as a psychiatrist as well as his status as an ordinary Black man and the consequent psychological effects of such treatment. French national culture ultimately proves to be exclusive. Its boundaries are, *prima facie*, more porous than race enabling a degree of mobility, but they are still maintained by members of the racially dominant group. Taken together, *Black Skin, White Masks* positions itself against anti-Black racism, French cultural chauvinism, and the latent restrictions of French citizenship more generally.

FRANTZ FANON (1925–61)

Frantz Fanon was a psychiatrist and philosopher who joined the Algerian liberation struggle against France during the 1950s. He is best known for two books, *Black Skin, White Masks* (1952) and *The Wretched of the Earth* (1961). Born in 1925 to a middle-class family on the Caribbean island of Martinique, he fought for the Free French forces against the Vichy Government and Nazi Germany during the Second World War. He returned to France after the war to study psychiatry at the University of Lyon. After holding several temporary posts in France, he moved to Algeria upon receiving a letter of appointment in October 1953 to work at the Blida-Joinville Hospital outside of Algiers. His residence there transformed his medical work and political commitments. The Algerian Revolution (1954–62) was among the longest anticolonial wars against the French, the French-Indochina War (1946–54) being of comparable length. In *The Wretched of the Earth*, Fanon argued that armed struggle against colonialism was indispensable, in addition to warning of the new dangers of a postcolonial elite taking power. Fanon's first book, *Black Skin, White Masks*, contrasts his last in a number of ways, consisting of a series of essays on topics including psychiatry, colonialism, Négritude, and the French policy of assimilation. It is a far more personal work than *The Wretched of the Earth*. Though often approached as a study of race and the effects of racism, it can also be read as a critique of the French idea and policy of assimilation, in which equality was attained through speaking French and embracing French cultural values. Fanon published a third book between his first and last, *L'An V de la Révolution algérienne* (1959, reprinted and translated as *A Dying Colonialism* in 1965), as well as numerous medical journal articles and political essays, a selection of which appear in the posthumous collections *Toward the African Revolution* (1964) and *Alienation and Freedom* (2015). His reputation as a vital interpreter of colonialism and anticolonialism remains undiminished. Fanon died from cancer at the age of 36, the same year as the publication of *The Wretched of the Earth*.

Cultural identity can, therefore, be a source of constraint and opportunity. For Appiah, it can be a positive source of identification and empowerment, a means of navigating a world of difference. On the other hand, it can be overdetermined as a source of identity, leading to limited agency and social exclusion. Like 'race' it is a condition that many people perceive as congenital—an identity that a person is born into. While there is truth to this observation—we are all born and raised in cultural settings—Appiah urges recognition for internal diversity within communities, how people inhabit multiple identities at once, and how some cultural identities may in fact be 'invented' (Hobsbawm et al. 2012 [1983]). 'Culture' can be as much a fiction as 'race'. But that is not to say that it is unimportant. Fictions have their uses. This chapter touches upon four key interventions Appiah has made on the question of culture and cultural identity: culture as an aesthetic resource; culture as temporality; culture as a critical stance; and culture as learned rather than inherited. Each of these engagements resembles a philosophical scenario with Appiah engaging with one or two specific thinkers. Indeed, he demonstrates an eclecticism of thought by discussing the arguments of writers, literary critics, anthropologists, sociologists, scholars of religion, and other intellectuals. Put simply, Appiah does not address 'culture' in a systematic way. Nonetheless, culture is a recurrent theme throughout Appiah's work. Like 'race', it contains inconsistencies, runs the risk of essentialization, and hence requires scrutiny.

'CULTURE' AND THE POSTCOLONIAL WRITER

One approach to the question of culture and cultural identity is to ask how artists and other cultural workers have negotiated this issue. In Chapter 4 of *In My Father's House*, entitled 'The Myth of an African World', Appiah focuses on the role of the writer. He draws specific attention to Wole Soyinka, the Nigerian playwright and Nobel Laureate, as an example of the promise and problem of 'culture'. He views Soyinka as 'the archetypical African writer' and considers his work a deliberation over culture and its uses (IMFH: 78). What are the contours and content of 'culture', and what functions—social, political, or otherwise—does it serve? The stature and work of Soyinka invite these questions, given his international audience, his writing in English, and his use of Yoruba culture and Nigerian history as source material. Soyinka, in sum, embodies an intersection of colonialism and postcolonialism, informed by Nigerian standards and international concerns alike. His life and creative work raise fundamental questions as to how 'culture' can be applied as an analytic concept and drawn from as a source of identity.

Appiah approaches these questions by setting up an initial contrast. The American literary critic Lionel Trilling (1905–75) once distinguished between 'sincerity' and 'authenticity' (Trilling 1972) to capture a shift in modern literature from a belief that the writer should express their subjective truth to society ('sincerity') to an understanding that the writer must express their subjective truth *against* social conventions and political ideologies ('authenticity'). The subsequent challenge for contemporary writers—assumed to be Euro-American in Trilling's argument—has been one of sustaining social criticism, of discovering a location of authenticity, typically on the margins, whereby a political vantage point can be maintained. In Appiah's assessment, African writers face a contrasting set of challenges. They are already perceived as outsiders, and their predicament has been 'finding a public role, not a private self' (IMFH: 76). Further complicating this task is a cultural past that has been hard for many African writers to shake—'their people's myths of the past are not things they can ignore'—thus reinforcing a cultural 'authenticity' that has been difficult to escape (IMFH: 76). In short, African writers find themselves marginalized and constrained by 'authenticity' in Trilling's political definition but also by its more general cultural definition—an opposite predicament to that encountered by Euro-American writers. Furthermore, if identity is a 'private problem' for the latter writer, it is often a public problem imposed on the African writer, who draws upon culture and history, but does not want to be restrained by them (IMHF: 76). Though both find themselves in the role of the social critic, the African writer and the Western writer are, in a sense, striving in opposite directions.

Soyinka provides a case study for examining this tension between 'individual self-discovery' and the 'social vision' (IMFH: 78). He has neither sought to relinquish his roles as an African writer and public intellectual, nor has he sacrificed his more subjective and private motivations. In a critical sketch of his play *Death and the King's Horseman* (1975), a tragedy involving the death of a father and son in colonial Nigeria, Appiah discusses how Soyinka resists the depiction of the play as a 'clash of cultures' between colonial and Yoruba values due to the insinuation of equivalence that such a formulation has. Appiah quotes Soyinka's statement, 'The Colonial Factor is an incident, a catalytic incident merely' (IMFH: 78). Yet Appiah also contends this disclaimer is misleading. The 'Colonial Factor' instead constitutes 'a profound assault on the consciousness of the African intellectual, on the consciousness that guides this play' (IMFH: 78). Though he agrees with Soyinka that equivalence between African and European perspectives is wrong, Appiah deems it 'irresponsible' for Soyinka to minimize this dynamic entirely. 'It is one thing to say (as I think correctly) that the drama in Oyo is driven ultimately by the logic of Yoruba cosmology', Appiah writes, 'another to deny the existence of a dimension of power in which it is the colonial state that forms the action' (IMFH: 78). Appiah sees this denial as an attempt by Soyinka to abscond his public role in favor of a more private set of ambitions. The question is why Soyinka 'feels the need to conceal his purposes', given this deflection betrays an unresolved dilemma between 'a private authenticity and a public commitment' (IMFH: 78).

Appiah finds a provisional answer to this question in Soyinka's book *Myth, Literature and the African World* (1976), based on a series of lectures delivered at Cambridge University. Of interest to Appiah is the question of audience for these lectures, and how Soyinka feels obligated to address Yoruba culture in a manner that is understandable to non-Yoruba people. On the one hand, Soyinka's approach underscores how African intellectuals cannot take culture for granted. It must be thoroughly explained, given the ignorance of many regarding African histories, cultures, and values. On the other hand, this explanatory impulse on the part of African writers in their non-fiction contrasts with their creative work. As Appiah notes, 'in Soyinka's plays Yoruba mythology and theology, Yoruba custom and tradition *are* taken for granted' (his emphasis, IMFH: 79). Appiah interprets this dualism as revealing how 'Africa' is understood by outsiders and the subsequent risks of reply. Soyinka's use of Yoruba culture as source material is at once natural, given his identity, but it also constrains him. Appiah believes that Soyinka, despite acknowledging cultural differences among African societies, resists the latter restriction by depicting for African audiences 'a deep and deeply self-conscious continuity between the problems and projects of [all] decolonized Africans'. This 'continuity' is 'both metaphysical and endogenous' (IMFH: 81). Soyinka, in short, goes in two directions at once—at times explaining 'Africa' to non-African audiences and mobilizing cultural detail in his plays to inoculate any slippage into generalization, while on other occasions working with general assumptions about the African condition at the metaphysical level.

This method, however skilled and intentional, can of course lead to inconsistency. Soyinka's conviction that a 'metaphysical consensus' exists among African cultures and societies is overdetermined and unwarranted in Appiah's eyes. 'I have insisted from the very beginning that the socio-historical situation of African writers generates a common set of problems', Appiah remarks, but this shared situation is not based on cultural unanimity, but is the outcome of European imperialism. More specifically, this condition is defined by 'the transition from traditional to modern loyalties; the experience of colonialism; [and] the racial theories and prejudices of Europe' (IMFH: 81). Though Soyinka's resistance to these outside factors is understandable, the turn to an 'endogenous account', whether Yoruba or another society, can have the effect of symbolizing 'Africa', thus becoming an accomplice to enduring Western perspectives about the uniformity of African culture. What Appiah calls 'the myth of Africa's metaphysical solidarity' can be seen as a postcolonial analog to the 19th-century inventions of Africa discussed in Chapter 1.

Appiah's assessment of Soyinka as a writer and intellectual is consequently one that is finely drawn—at once praising his use and foregrounding of local cultural perspectives, but also highlighting the dangers of overgeneralizing African culture from such circumstances. Soyinka himself is aware of these risks in relation to what he sees as the errors of other Black intellectuals. Indeed, he addresses this danger of homogenizing 'Africa' in his critique of Négritude, a discussion also found in *Myth, Literature and the African World*. It is unclear why Appiah does not credit him with this point. What is clear is that the role and challenges that African writers and other cultural workers face are different from those confronted by writers in the West as described by Trilling. The African writer is already a marginal figure. 'Authenticity' in both cultural and political senses can be a burden and a constriction, rather than an aspirational principle. Culture as a source for art and identification is therefore not as straightforward as it might first appear, raising questions of representation, responsibility, and individual agency for the writer and artist.

THE 'NONTRADITIONAL'

Soyinka's working notion of an 'African metaphysical solidarity' (IMFH: 82), though opposed to Eurocentrism, is not the only approach that reflects the latent pervasiveness of monolithic European understandings of 'Africa'. Another frame that imparts essentialism is the topos of the 'modern' and the 'traditional', as addressed in Appiah's chapter 'Old Gods, New Worlds' from *In My Father's House*—an intervention that attempts to break this clichéd framework. These temporal identities with their attendant political and cultural attributes have differentiated 'Africa' from 'the West' in problematic ways. As the anthropologist Johannes Fabian has argued in *Time and the Other* (1983), 'allochronism' (asynchronicity), whereby Europe is seen as 'ahead' of other parts of the world, has been a persistent method for distinguishing the West and diminishing the Rest (Fabian 1983).

With regard to the 'modern', Appiah asserts there should be a common set of interests between Western and African intellectuals on this issue—the 'modern', after all, assumes a mutual present. There is, in fact, a fundamental difference. For Euro-American intellectuals, being modern is taken for granted, a 'fait accompli' as Appiah puts it. For African intellectuals, this situation does not exist. They are driven instead by the question of how 'our cultures are to *become* modern' (his emphasis, IMFH: 107). Appiah is unsurprisingly critical of this longstanding structure of temporal inequality that conveys a sense of permanent belatedness for African societies. As a provisional solution, he maps an intermediate ground by taking account of the effects of a European colonialism that created 'a culture in transition from tradition to modernity', which he refers to as being 'nontraditional' (IMFH: 107).

Religion provides a way for Appiah to demonstrate this intermediate position of the 'nontraditional'. Drawing on the example of an Asante ceremony involving ritual animal sacrifice in order to install a spirit (*obosom*) in a shrine, Appiah discusses how 'traditional' religious practices endure in the present (IMFH:

108,109). To explain this situation, he references an influential argument by Geertz who characterized religion as a 'system of symbols': unequivocal belief is not always indispensable to maintaining certain ritual practices (IMFH: 112). Yet this explanation does not account for orthodox believers. Symbolism can still reflect committed religious belief. An alternative approach for understanding the endurance of traditional religious practices in Africa is to consider religious ritual and symbolism in 'modern' societies. Regarding the decline of religious ceremony in industrialized countries, Appiah writes that the importance of religious belief has not subsided, only that ceremonial accouterments can arguably be witnessed more conspicuously in 'traditional' societies. Surface differences between 'traditional' and 'modern' societies can therefore be misleading. Both societies are in transition and are 'nontraditional'. 'Prayer has become for many [in the industrialized West] like an intimate conversation', Appiah concludes. 'But so it is for Asante tradition. It is just that the understanding of intimacy is different' (IMFH: 115).

This comparison, which clearly risks overgeneralization, leads to a deeper question. If 'modern' societies retain 'traditional' systems of belief, which in different ways work against modern forms of secular reason, why is this so? Why does religious faith persist in the face of modern science? Appiah resorts to sociologist Émile Durkheim (1858–1917) for one provisional answer. To paraphrase Durkheim, if it is true that false beliefs do not last, then existing beliefs must be understood to be taken as true, and they must be perceived as true on a symbolic basis if not on a literal basis. This argument is akin to Geertz's. A Catholic who partakes in communion does not literally believe that the communion wafer is the body of Christ, but they still devoutly believe in the symbolic importance of this understanding to their faith and Catholic identity. In this regard, upbringing can be as important as consistency of belief. Citing the work of British anthropologist E. E. Evans-Pritchard (1902–73), Appiah asserts that we accept certain beliefs because we are born into certain cultures and learn these beliefs at a young age. Having these beliefs does not necessarily make them true. But childhood and cultural upbringing can powerfully impact an individual's identification with belief systems well into adulthood.

Appiah therefore does not call such believers 'unreasonable' (IMFH: 118). Rather, he sees secular and religious forms of reason as performing similar roles in explaining the world. To illustrate this point, he draws an analogy between religious faith and the modern natural sciences, both of which share a methodological approach that he summarizes as 'explanation, prediction, and control' (IMFH: 118). When scientists fail to prove a certain theory, they do not reinvent their discipline or disband their field entirely. They instead make revisions to their ideas or conduct further experiments to verify arguments through empirical results. Positions can often be too 'theory-laden' and need more evidence. Scientific theories can therefore be 'underdetermined', but not necessarily false. 'If we gave up every time an experiment failed, scientific theory would get nowhere', Appiah summarizes (IMFH: 119). Taken further, religious thought adjusts in the same way as scientific thought. For Appiah, the main difference between African religious thought and Western scientific thought is that the former is 'couched in terms of personal forces' while the latter is 'couched in terms of impersonal forces' (IMFH: 121). Engaging the work of religion scholar Robin Horton (1932–2019), Appiah further elaborates that 'traditional' religions invoke 'theoretical entities' as agents of change and explanation rather than 'material forces', which predominate explanations of causality in modern societies (IMFH: 122).

Where Appiah ultimately finds common ground and a means of breaking from the 'traditional' and 'modern' distinction is through a discussion of 'open' and 'closed' societies. Horton believed that 'traditional' societies are 'closed' whereas 'modern' societies are 'open', a point with which Appiah disagrees. As he comments,

> It is ... the availability of alternative theories of morals and nature that gives rise to the systematic investigation of nature, to the growth of speculation, and to the development of that crucial element that distinguishes the open society—namely, organized challenges to prevailing theory.
>
> (IMFH: 125)

This 'availability of alternative theories' has not been unique to the modern period. Traditional societies were equally exposed to new ideas and beliefs through trade and political expansion. Appiah notes that Horton revised his stance to say that traditional societies were 'accommodative' (IMFH: 127), with the orality of precolonial traditions enabling this accommodation. Yet, more significant for Appiah was the introduction of written literacy that resulted from this openness, which, in turn, enabled scientific thinking through systematic critical analysis. The written word was more stable than the spoken word, permitting concrete debate and security of understanding at the same time. As Appiah summarizes, literacy was a crucial step, even if it was not in itself 'sufficient to make for science' (IMFH: 131–32). 'Write, then, and the demands imposed by the distant, unknown reader require more universality, more abstraction', Appiah insists.

> Because our reader may not share the cultural assumptions necessary to understand them, in contexts where communication of information is central our written language becomes less figurative. And so another nail is beaten into the coffin of the inconsistencies of our informal thought.
> (IMFH: 132)

Though critics have argued that oral literatures possess a rigor equivalent to written literatures, Appiah contends that literacy, with its unique form of critical reasoning, revolutionized Asante society as it has African societies more generally. And yet traditional practices still persist. There remains the issue of 'becoming', of cultures 'in transition', as noted at the start of this section. He concludes that there are ultimately two issues at stake for addressing the condition of the 'nontraditional': 'a practical one' for African intellectuals and 'a moral one' for non-Africans (IMFH: 134). Regarding the former, intellectuals will continue to engage in critical analysis enabled by literacy. 'This process of analysis will produce new, unpredictable, fusions', he writes (IMFH: 134). Regarding the latter, Appiah criticizes once more non-African views that overemphasize traditional practices in African societies and position them as purely symbolic and unreasonable. 'Concentrating on the noncognitive features of traditional religions not only misrepresents them', he further remarks, 'but also leads to an underestimation of the role of reason in the life of traditional cultures' (IMFH: 134). Though he does censure the unthinking aspects of traditional belief—its intermittent rejection of Western medicine, for example—his concern is ultimately to defend African traditional beliefs from Western criticism. In his final defense, he invokes a philosophical position of Kwasi Wiredu. 'We will only solve our problems if we see them as human problems arising out of a special situation', Appiah summarizes, 'and we shall not solve them if we see them as African problems, generated by our being somehow unlike others' (IMFH: 136). The dichotomy of the 'traditional' and 'modern' therefore threatens more than simply chronologizing conditions in Africa. It fosters identities of cultural difference between 'Africa' and 'the West' that must be rescinded by both African and non-African societies alike (see also Gyekye 1997; Janz 2009).

THE POSTMODERN AND THE POSTCOLONIAL

Appiah's essay 'Is the Post- in Postmodernism the Post- in Postcolonial?' (1991), which first appeared in the journal *Critical Inquiry* and was later included in *In My Father's House*, marks yet another engagement with culture—in this instance, culture as supplying a critical stance. Though this framing can already be seen in the preceding discussions, this essay brings this element more clearly into the foreground. It is one of Appiah's best-known pieces. As its title suggests, it is a key intervention in the relationship between postmodernism and postcolonialism, which both gained popularity in academic circles during the 1980s. The essay's interstitial quality, residing between fields and discussions, is characteristic of Appiah. It is fixated once more on the question of cultural identity. Though related to the temporal issues of the 'traditional' and the 'modern', the argument on this occasion regards the question of whether the terms 'postmodern' or 'postcolonial' provide new forms of artistic identification and intellectual agency.

Appiah begins his essay by describing an African art exhibition held in New York in 1987 titled 'Perspectives: Angles on African Art'. He uses this event to untangle the tense intersections between Western critics and African artists, commodity value and artistic ambition, 'traditional' aesthetics and the 'modern' present. Appiah focuses in particular on a piece chosen by the exhibition's co-curator, the African-American writer James Baldwin (1924–87), whose selection of a Yoruba sculpture entitled *Man with a Bicycle* went against the 'primitive' aesthetic deemed more authentic by Western critics. This artwork serves as a point of orientation for Appiah's digressive musings on 'postmodernism' and 'postcolonialism'.

Both terms are slippery in usage and meaning, and Appiah does not seek to bridge or fuse the two together. Rather, he places them in dialogue to understand their affinities and frictions. He writes how both constitute a 'space-clearing gesture' intended to think beyond what came before (Appiah 1991b: 348, 356). 'Postmodernism' as defined by the French philosopher Jean-François Lyotard is, in Appiah's words, 'a metanarrative of the end of metanarratives' (IMFH: 140; Lyotard 1979). While Appiah's summary underlines his view that postmodernism maintains intrinsic contradictions by celebrating multiplicity while using a single concept to do so, he is more critical of its temporal framing and generational antagonism. 'Lyotard's postmodernism—his theorization of contemporary life as postmodern', Appiah writes, 'is *after* modernism because it rejects aspects of modernism' (his emphasis, IMFH: 141). In this sense, postmodernism has little to offer except an a posteriori attitude of retroactive judgment. Fredric Jameson's approach (Jameson 1991) to the term provides a compelling alternative by addressing mass commodification as a key factor in defining the conditions of postmodernity and the different formal (high) and informal (low) aesthetics that have attended it (IMFH: 142). Still, Appiah believes these discussions leave unanswered questions as to how these theories relate to temporality and life itself—in his words, 'the relations between postmodern*ism* and postmodern*ity*' (his emphasis, IMFH: 142). What do these terms mean for the individual?

Part of the problem is 'modernity' itself. Appiah cites the work of Max Weber as one source of definition. Weber characterized modernity by its tendency toward rationalization, whether through scientific or humanistic reason. He referred to this process as contributing to the 'disenchantment of the world' (Weber 1919). Yet Appiah sees Weber's argument as unrealized. The persistence of traditional reason in the form of religious thought, as discussed earlier, demonstrates that the world continues to be 'enchanted' in different ways. While Appiah admits that Western modernity has 'a universal *geographical* significance', given the global influence of Western culture, he also judges that 'the rationalization of the world can no longer be seen as the tendency either of the West or of history' (his emphasis, IMFH: 144). 'To understand our world is to reject Weber's claim for the rationality of what he called rationalization and his projection of its inevitability', Appiah concludes. As such, it is necessary to consider 'a radically post-Weberian conception of modernity' that accommodates societies and forms of reason beyond Europe (IMFH: 145).

Like postmodernism, postcolonialism also presents thorny problems of definition. Does postcolonialism refer to a condition, a process, or a temporality? 'For the *post* in postcolonial, like the *post* in postmodern[,] is the *post* of the space-clearing gesture I characterized earlier', Appiah argues. He additionally writes, 'Postcoloniality is *after* all this: and its *post*, like postmodernism's, is also a *post* that challenges earlier legitimating narratives' (his emphasis, IMFH: 155). Yet 'many areas of contemporary African cultural life—what has come to be theorized as popular culture, in particular—are not in this way concerned with transcending, with going beyond, coloniality' (IMFH: 149). In this instance, Appiah contradicts his insistence on the shallow impact of colonialism discussed in Chapter 1 of this book. Similar to his critique of Soyinka, he demands consideration of colonialism's continued legacies. He re-emphasizes how 'postcolonial' intellectuals and cultural artifacts, such as *Man with a Bicycle*, can be indebted to both 'colonial' influences and 'traditional' aesthetics. Furthermore, like postmodernism, there are multiple approaches for addressing the tone, ambition, outlook, and content of postcolonialism. These approaches include post-nativist, post-national, post-realist, and post-optimistic viewpoints. Appiah, therefore, sees postcolonialism as a critical position similar to postmodernism, though for him it is more significant due to its potential to challenge Eurocentrism 'in the name of the ethical universal; in the name of *humanism*' (his emphasis, IMFH: 155). Indeed, he sees postcolonialism as 'not an ally for Western postmodernism' but an 'agonist', an interlocutor or combatant, from which 'postmodernism may have something to learn' (IMFH: 155).

The 'post' in 'postmodern' and the 'post' in 'postcolonial' do not ultimately designate a shared methodological agenda or chronological timing, as examined and maintained by some scholars (Ahluwalia 2010). Appiah emphasizes how canonical postcolonial novels like Chinua Achebe's *Things Fall Apart* (1958) or Camara Laye's *L'Enfant noir* (1953) written during the late colonial period are textbook examples of modernism, rather than postmodernism, through their departures from local aesthetic traditions and their concerns for realism. Instead, the prefix 'post' in Appiah's purview is designed and better utilized to interrogate the question of boundaries—political, historical, and cultural. In both instances, it creates a provisional 'problemspace' (Scott 1999) for wrestling with matters of epochal continuity and difference that relate to historical change, like political decolonization, yet are not overdetermined by such transitions either. Culture possesses its own temporality that does not always align with politics.

Identity is also at stake. To interpret 'postcolonial' cultural artifacts, whether art or writing, as also being 'postmodern' due to their disregard for realism or narrative conventions runs the risk of neglecting stances like 'post-nativism' and 'post-optimism' that an African author or artist may be articulating (Appiah 1991: 353). Against this application of outside frameworks to African aesthetics, Appiah additionally highlights the African contributions to Western modernism—witnessed, for example, in the 'primitive' aesthetic of Pablo Picasso's *Les Demoiselles d'Avignon* (1907). He also cites the hazard of African artists becoming 'otherness machines', to use an expression of Sara

Suleri, whereby artistic production is a matter of meeting a market demand for the 'primitive' or 'exotic' (Appiah 1991: 356; Suleri 1989). In the end, Appiah rests his case on the limits of theory and the importance of the identity and imagination of the individual artist. 'What happens will happen not because we pronounce on the matter in theory', Appiah concludes, 'but will happen out of the changing everyday practices of African cultural life' (Appiah 1991: 356).

DU BOIS AND LEARNED CULTURE

Culture and cultural identity are not solely matters of birth or childhood upbringing. They can also be learned, appropriated, and adapted for different uses. Appiah addresses this possibility in *Lines of Descent: W. E. B. Du Bois and the Emergence of Identity* (2014), his book about Du Bois's time in Berlin as a graduate student from 1892 to 1894. Based on a series of lectures Appiah delivered at Harvard, the purpose of revisiting this brief, but foundational, time in Du Bois's life is to discern the intellectual wellspring of his later writings on race, Pan-Africanism, and Black identity. This engagement marks a return for Appiah to rethink his earlier examination of Du Bois outlined in the previous chapter. In contrast to the philosophical tussle in 'Illusions of Race', Appiah undertakes a biographical approach that situates a wider horizon for understanding Du Bois and his range of commitments. Appiah argues that the lessons of culture and historicism he internalized while studying in Berlin were vital to his development. 'Du Bois was America's last romantic', Appiah writes with a flourish. 'Du Bois's arguments were tethered to the varieties of racial romanticism and postromantic thought that he took from Germany's intellectual traditions' (LD: 22).

Du Bois's fascination with Germany was not unusual—several of his teachers at Harvard, including the philosophers William James (1842–1910) and George Santayana (1863–1952), had either studied or spent considerable time there—but it does illuminate the sources of his racial thinking. Du Bois encountered an intellectual climate that sought to produce academic knowledge with political implications. The industrialization of

Europe during the 19th century had generated inequalities that drew the attention of social scientists. Gustav von Schmoller (1838–1917), an economic historian and founder of the *Verein für Sozialpolitik* (Association for Social Policy), believed that scholarship could be 'both dispassionate and engaged' (LD: 31). As Appiah puts it, Schmoller and his colleagues 'didn't think that the ethical could be excluded from historical studies, not least because the development of the ethical was itself a historical phenomenon' (LD: 33). This approach found its way into Du Bois's thinking. Not only could the 'Social Question' (*die Soziale Frage*) be translated to the 'Negro Question' (*Negerfrage*) (Du Bois 2006 [1906]), but methods of analysis could also be transferred. Schmoller and other members of the *Verein* criticized the idea that social progress could be attributed to 'timeless natural laws' or be the result of pure individualism (LD: 38, 39). Social classes and systemic conditions mattered. This historicism intersected with Du Bois's embrace of German Romanticism—specifically, Johann Gottfried Herder (1744–1803), whose concept of the spiritual character of nations (*Volkgeist*) deeply impacted Du Bois's Pan-Africanism. Notions of 'striving' (*streben*) and 'soul' (*geist*) would surface directly in *The Souls of Black Folk*.

Appiah underscores how these notions informed Du Bois's worldview. Berlin enabled him to see the American situation of race from a distance—a condition of racial exile. As Appiah remarks, 'Germany was the first place where Du Bois experienced life without the daily cruelties and public insults of racism' (LD: 28). Du Bois himself, as quoted by Appiah, plainly stated, 'this was the land where I first met white folk who treated me as a human being' (LD: 28). Du Bois later reflected on this emergent global outlook in *The Souls of Black Folk*, stressing that the problem of the 'color-line' included 'men in Asia and Africa, in America and the islands of the sea' (Du Bois 1986: 372). This intellectual eclecticism in Du Bois's thought further elucidates the blending of the personal and the social in his later writing. This 'disciplinary schizophrenia' can be witnessed in his oscillation between 'soaring, rhapsodic poeticism and dry, assiduous empiricism', reflecting the influence of another German scholar whom Du Bois studied under, Wilhelm Dilthey (1833–1911), and his distinction between the impulse to explain (*erklären*) and the need to understand (*verstehen*) (LD: 78, 79). For Appiah, this tension between clarifying facts and understanding souls underlies Du Bois's question from *The Souls of Black Folk*: 'How does it feel to be a problem?' (LD: 82)

These influences ultimately contributed to and legitimated Du Bois's sociohistorical approach to race. Franz Boas had left for the United States from the Royal Ethnographic Museum in Berlin only a few years before Du Bois's arrival. Du Bois later invited him to deliver a commencement address at Atlanta University in 1906, after Boas had become a professor at Columbia University and Du Bois had received a faculty position at Atlanta. Beyond their agreement on the pseudoscience of race, both were united on the issue of culture. As Appiah writes, 'cultural transmission' became a central feature of Du Bois's understanding of race (LD: 108). But equal to this theme for Du Bois was the role of politics. Appiah argues that Du Bois's recurrent engagement with 'race' and its definition did not exclusively comprise 'an attempt to reflect the existing reality of race' but constituted 'an attempt to call his own race to action' (LD: 113). 'Du Bois moved on from the biology and the anthropology of the nineteenth century', Appiah concludes, 'but he never left its world of idealistic ethical nationalism' (LD: 113).

European culture was not the only cultural influence Du Bois explored. The foregrounding of culture and embrace of an 'idealistic ethical nationalism' required history, specifically a Pan-African history that included the African continent. Even though Du Bois's first book concerned the suppression of the transatlantic slave trade (Du Bois 1986), Appiah notes that Du Bois did not write directly about Africa's past until much later. Though he touched upon the matter of cultural 'retentions' and 'survivals' (Mintz and Price 1992: 52, 53) with a discussion of 'long-formed habits' in *The Negro Church* (1903), Du Bois's engagement with African history did not begin in earnest until the publication of *The Negro* (1915) and later—after his visits to Liberia, Sierra Leone, and Senegal (1923–24)—with the books *Africa, Its Geography, People and Products* (1930) and *Africa—Its Place in Modern History* (1930). As Appiah underscores, Du Bois's first visit to the African continent had an effect similar to the one he experienced in Germany, where he found 'a land where his racial identity lost its salience' (LD: 139). An unexpected consequence of this experience is that rather than reinforcing his ideas of Blackness, his time in Africa contributed to the dissolution of certain long-held ideas. Black culture was not a single entity. 'Either way, if he hoped to learn about himself by learning about Africa—by a profound immersion in its cultures and history—the result was paradoxical', Appiah writes, 'By installments, his studies of Africa served to complicate rather than clarify his sense of the Negro' (LD: 139).

Appiah concludes *Lines of Descent* by maintaining that the ideas Du Bois encountered in Germany continued to influence Du Bois's thinking. By extension, they have influenced present-day approaches to race. Appiah is less critical of Du Bois on this occasion than he was in 'Illusions of Race'. He is more sympathetic to the constraints Du Bois faced in his lifetime, as well as the multiple intellectual strands that he sought to weave together over the course of his career. There are missing figures that deserve mention. German thinkers who go underexamined or unexamined entirely include Marx and Friedrich Nietzsche (1844–1900). The latter's idea of the *Übermensch* likely informed Du Bois's promotion of an elite 'Talented Tenth' for leading racial uplift (Du Bois 1996a; Du Bois 1996b; Gates, Jr., and West 1996). Marx had a more conspicuous imprint, as seen in the Marxist analysis of *Black Reconstruction*, Du Bois's travels to the Soviet Union beginning in 1926, and his membership in the communist party at the end of his life. Another strange omission in Appiah's study is the Berlin Conference and German colonialism in Africa, which Du Bois must have been aware of before his arrival in Berlin.

Nonetheless, Appiah displays a reappraised view of Du Bois when he affirms the important contributions of Du Bois with regard to Black cultural history and how 'stories *do* bind people together so that they can accomplish shared goals' (his emphasis, LD: 161). There should be 'no barrier to full engagement with those narratives' even if 'your own particular ancestors were elsewhere when the events they record occurred' (LD: 161). This view revises his previous position against descent-based arguments, fictive or otherwise, to acknowledge cultural and intellectual forms of descent, as the title of his book itself indicates. For the purpose of this chapter, Appiah's re-examination of Du Bois is not only a project in historical restoration, but an argument about the diverse sources of cultural identity. As discussed in the first pages of *Lines of Descent*, 'the horizontal, peer-to-peer aspects of education' (LD: 4, 5) can be vital for identity formation—a complement to whatever circumstances a person is born into. The cosmopolitanism of Du Bois's education deeply informed his project of defining Black identity without resorting to monocausal explanations of science, history, culture, or politics. The color line was not the only line to influence Du Bois's thinking. The method of social constructionism that he pioneered was the result of his engaged research imagination and his creative interweaving of multiple intellectual strands from different cultural contexts. Academic ideas and the personal narratives they fostered could also 'bind people together'. They granted Du Bois a cultural world and freedom of mind he might not have experienced otherwise.

CONCLUSIONS

In *The Lies that Bind*, Appiah discusses the notion of *habitus*, popularized by the French sociologist Pierre Bourdieu (1930–2002), which argues that cultural habits are not only learned early in one's life, but they are internalized such that we perform them, bodily and otherwise, without consciously thinking. Cultural identity is an identity that we can be accustomed to without giving it a second thought. However, as discussed in this chapter, culture is a source of identity that requires critical engagement, whether it is a form of inheritance, as in the case of Soyinka, or something that is learned from mentors and peers, as in the case of Du Bois. Like race, culture contains its own fictional attributes which must be negotiated, whether socio-temporal frameworks of the 'traditional' and the 'modern' or related critical stances of the 'postcolonial' and the 'postmodern'. There is also a truth to culture, particularly in its locally lived manifestations, that Appiah embraces. He does not deconstruct it in the same way he does 'race', with the purpose of ending a Eurocentric epistemology for understanding the world and, from a political standpoint, eliminating an idea that has harmed individuals and communities, often violently, for centuries. Rather, culture possesses its own challenges for both constraining and enabling identity and individual freedom, the latter of which will be examined further in the next chapter.

4

LIBERALISM

Liberalism is about individual freedom. Though there are varieties of liberal thought, different concepts of liberty, and debates over social justice, liberalism as a political philosophy can be reduced to this principal idea. It is a tradition that has both enabled and limited the expression of identity. As discussed throughout the last several chapters, Appiah is critical of the use of certain identities. His concern is rooted in his role as a philosopher and his commitments to truth and reason. He is firm in his belief regarding the role of intellectuals to address 'these fictions in our lives', believing 'the institutionalization of this imperative in the academy' amounts to a social good (IMFH: 178–79). Yet, Appiah accepts that identity groups do not often heed the opinions of academic philosophers. Given their political uses, these fictions must be taken seriously. What role do identities play in politics? How should identities be treated in relation to questions of civic duty, equality, and social justice? How does individual autonomy relate to group identities, and what role, if any, should states have? This chapter explores these questions. Though identities may have their fictive qualities, they still impact our lives.

The Ethics of Identity (2005) focuses on these issues. It is an expansive work that provides a guided tour of liberal thought, while making a case for its continuation at the start of the 21st century in the wake of the Cold War and the ideological conflicts of the 20th century. Appiah's title refers to the ethics of identification for individuals, as well as the ethics of addressing people of other identities, whether by states through law and social policy or by other identity groups and their members. In this regard, liberalism is also about 'pluralism'—the fact that we live with people that are different from us. Unlike the more popular expressions 'identity politics' or 'the politics of identity', his title insists on the moral foundations of identity. Ethical considerations should come before politics. Ethics, as Appiah defines the term, is 'the name we give to philosophical reflection on morality', with concepts and the moral implications of concepts up for scrutiny (TT: 178). Identity is one such concept for Appiah. His scholarship therefore does not solely regard the deconstruction of identities as seen previously. It is also about identifying the conditions of freedom for the individual and constructing moral societies that will enable that freedom—to achieve *eudaemonia*, to use Aristotle's term for 'living well' (TT: 216)—through and beyond identity.

LIBERALISM AFTER EMPIRE

Among the most prominent influences on Appiah's thought, especially in *The Ethics of Identity*, is John Stuart Mill. Appiah notes that Mill is the 'totem' of his book (EI: 271). Appiah works with him and against him. Mill is a complex influence, given his defense of colonialism in *On Liberty* (1859) as a type of 'benevolent despotism'. Yet Mill's project also argued for individual rights against the power of the state. As mentioned in Chapter 1, these concerns reflected a generational outlook. Born in 1806, Mill came of age in the wake of the French, American, and Haitian revolutions, which faced the resurgence of post-revolutionary state power epitomized by Napoleon Bonaparte (1769–1821). Like his near-contemporary Marx (born in 1818), Mill sought to build upon the ideas of the preceding generation's revolutions and address a post-revolutionary political order. His trajectory led him to a politics based on individual rights rather than Marx's ethos of revolutionary class struggle and its emancipatory potential.

Though Marx is not absent from Appiah's body of work, the reasons for his adoption of Mill may also reflect a generational disenchantment with ideologies of decolonization and the failures of African socialism. Like many anti-colonial nationalists, Nkrumah was deeply influenced by Marxism-Leninism, best seen in his book *Neo-Colonialism: The Last Stage of Imperialism* (1965), whose very title echoes Lenin's *Imperialism: The Highest Stage of Capitalism* (1917). But Appiah's preference can be attributed to Mill himself. Appiah writes in *The Ethics of Identity* that Mill 'had no love for theocrats and despots, for ways of life where individuality was stifled' (EI: 143). Appiah elaborates his own skepticism toward the politics of postcolonial Ghana in the chapter 'Altered States' from *In My Father's House*. He writes how the early period of independence under Nkrumah witnessed an enthusiastic 'allegiance to the Ghanaian state' because 'it was clear what it was that we were *against*—namely, British imperialism' (his emphasis, IMFH: 160). However, this energy soon dissipated. 'By 1966, when the first of our many postindependence [*sic*] coups exiled Nkrumah', Appiah reflects, 'the real, if limited, enthusiasm there once had been had largely evaporated and the complications began to take up our attention' (IMFH: 161). Against this backdrop, Appiah considers 'how surprising it is that there was a moment of "nationalism" at all' (IMFH: 161). Colonial rule had created a template for territorial nationalism, but one that encountered ethnic, cultural, and economic forms of diversity that posed obstacles for national cohesion. 'If the history of metropolitan Europe in the last century and a half has been a struggle to establish statehood for nationalities', Appiah writes, 'Europe left Africa at independence with states looking for nations' (IMFH: 162).

This disjuncture between national identity and local diversity generated political cynicism among Ghanaians. It also supplied a foundation for Appiah's engagement with political liberalism and what can be called his refinement of a 'postcolonial liberalism'. His embrace of this tradition was not purely academic. In another personal reflection from *In My Father's House*, he discusses a period during the mid-1970s when 'the Ghanaian state began its precipitous decline' and he happened to be teaching *Leviathan* (1651) by Thomas Hobbes (1588–1679) as part of a course in political philosophy at the University of Ghana. Despite 'the withdrawal of the Ghanaian state', a Hobbesian situation of chaos did not transpire. 'Ghanaian life was not a brutish war of all against all', he recalls. 'Life went on ... people made deals, bought and sold goods, owned houses, married, raised families' (IMFH: 168). He attributes this persistence in the absence of state stability to 'the regulation of life through the shared and intelligible norms that grew out of the responses of precolonial cultures to their engagement with European imperialism' (IMFH: 168). As he summarizes, postcolonial governments 'will have to learn something about the surprising persistence of these "premodern" affiliations, the cultural and political fretwork of relations through which our very identity is conferred' (IMFH: 171).

The point here is not only Appiah's belief in the capacity of civil society as a supplement and bulwark against state failure, but also the significant role of identities and their networks in constituting civil society. Though 'civil society' has been debated among political scientists, Appiah's observations can be situated within a broader liberal tradition, particularly in relation to diversity. Mill once more is unavoidable. As Appiah writes in *The Ethics of Identity*, Mill's antecedents, in particular Hobbes, were skeptical of diversity. It was 'a problem to be solved, not a condition to be promoted' (EI: 142). 'It is only with Mill that a sense of diversity as something that might be of value enters into mainstream Anglo-American political thought', Appiah continues (EI: 142). Mill envisioned diversity as an 'anterior fact' to be accommodated, but also a value to be cultivated through 'experiments of living'. In Appiah's words, 'diversity would beget diversity, for a population exposed to a variation of circumstances would grow more various' (EI: 142).

There are problems with Mill's conclusions, chief among them his argument in the long-form essay *On Liberty* in support of colonial rule as briefly touched upon earlier. 'Despotism is a legitimate mode of government in dealing with barbarians, provided the end be their improvement, and the means justified by actually effecting that end', he writes in the essay's introduction (Mill 1869: 23). Mill worked for the British East India Company for 35 years, starting at the age of 17. His father, James Mill (1773–1836), was an economist and historian who published *The History of British India* (1817), which conveyed disparaging views of India and rationalized the colonial governance of the British East India Company there. The younger Mill's career as a company administrator ended only when the British government took over the company in 1858 in the aftermath of the Indian Rebellion of 1857. Overall, as historian Dipesh Chakrabarty has allegorized in *Provincializing Europe* (2000), Mill's ideas effectively denied the rights and interests of colonized subjects, depicting them as unready for self-rule and relegating them to 'an imaginary waiting room of history' (Chakrabarty 2000: 8).

Scholars have interrogated Mill's rationalization of colonialism, which is also outlined in the essay 'A Few Words on Non-Intervention' (1859). In his book *Liberalism and Empire* (1999), the political philosopher Uday Singh Mehta has discussed how Mill, his father, and other liberal thinkers, such as Edmund Burke (1729–97), Jeremy Bentham (1748–1832), and Henry Maine (1822–88), were all deeply influenced by imperialism and British colonial rule in India in their formulation of individualism and the role of the state in guaranteeing or limiting rights. Jennifer Pitts has further elaborated this line of argument in her book *A Turn to Empire* (2005), first by mapping a different genealogy to include Alexis de Tocqueville (1805–59), but also by arguing that a number of early British thinkers, including Adam Smith (1723–90), were in fact critical of the politics of empire. The liberal embrace of imperialism did not take place until the 1830s.

Against this backdrop, Appiah mounts a provisional defense of Mill through the latter's criticism of slavery, which Mill described as a 'scourge to humanity' (EI: 145). Britain had abolished its trade in 1807 and ended the practice itself by 1834, in contrast to the United States and other parts of the world where slavery still continued. Appiah sees this critique as part of Mill's 'monism' (EI: 144–45)—a philosophical term referring to 'singularity', in this instance a single framework for the world and the rights of individuals. Yet an inconsistency remains. If the rights of the enslaved deserve to be recognized, why not the rights of the colonized? The philosopher Charles Mills has been critical of the liberal tradition for this inconsistency, arguing that liberalism, consciously or not, has been defined by white domination, colonial and otherwise, resulting in what he terms 'racial liberalism'—an expression meant to undo the colorblindness of liberalism (Mills 2017: 6).

While this debate over Mill cannot be completely resolved in this book, what is clear is that Appiah has drawn on his ideas and those of other thinkers, liberal or not, as tools in his search for answers about the ethics of identity. Appiah is not preoccupied with judging Mill and others from a historical standpoint. As he puts it in the essay 'Liberalism, Individuality, and Identity' (2001), he is more concerned with the philosophical foundations, rather than the historical foundations, of the liberal tradition. A detractor might still claim he is not critical enough, that he is conceding to an intrinsically Eurocentric point of view, despite his admonishment of Eurocentrism on other occasions. A more generous critic might say that Appiah is appropriating, extending, and redefining liberalism through his own work. Certainly, his engagement with liberalism is distinctive, if not entirely unique, among African philosophers. Rather than being a credulous proponent, Appiah is a critical interlocutor within the tradition, cultivating a 'postcolonial liberalism' informed by his Ghanaian background. *The Ethics of Identity* is his boldest attempt at amending liberalism for the present and future.

INDIVIDUALISM

The Ethics of Identity touches upon a number of subjects that have preoccupied Appiah's thinking—race, culture, identity—while also presenting summary discussions of how to approach these topics from an ethical standpoint. Unlike *In My Father's House*, which is largely concerned with deconstructing certain identities, and later works like *Lines of Descent*, which is an intellectual history, this book is about *practice*—how to engage the world proactively. It prescribes the application of ethics to individual decision-making in order to contribute to a broader moral purpose within one's community. Appiah adheres to a distinction made by legal scholar Ronald Dworkin (1931–2013) in which the term 'ethics' applies to individuals and their decision-making ('self-regarding'), while the term 'morality' applies to the treatment of other people ('other-regarding') (EI: xiii; TT: 215–17). Appiah states that his book is not a work of political theory (EI: xvii). Nonetheless, it is an argument for revisiting and reviving the liberal tradition after the Cold War and at the start of a new century.

LIBERALISM AND LITERATURE

The liberal political tradition may appear to have little to offer students of literature. Yet, recent scholarship has demonstrated the concurrent rise of the novel and the concept of human rights. In *Inventing Human Rights: A History* (2007), Lynn Hunt, a historian of revolutionary France, has written how the concept of rights that became the basis of the Declaration of the Rights of Man and of the Citizen (1789) was influenced by artistic production during the 18th century, including visual portraiture and the novel. She specifically cites Samuel Richardson's *Pamela* (1740) and Jean-Jacques Rousseau's *Julie* (1761) as examples of literary works whose emphasis on personhood contributed to ideas of natural rights and empathy for other people through those rights. In *Human Rights, Inc.* (2007), Joseph Slaughter has made a parallel argument regarding the *Bildungsroman* form and modern human rights discourse as being mutually connected to longstanding developments emerging from the Enlightenment to address and civilize the world. He also discusses how this connection has been an ambivalent one, as the novel has been complicit with modern imperialism in terms of negating the rights, social relations, and desire for self-determination among the colonized. In summary, these interventions by Hunt and Slaughter only briefly described here highlight the ways in which liberalism as a political philosophy with attention to individual rights can be utilized for literary analysis.

Mill's views on the importance of liberty and freedom of expression for the individual, which can lead to truth and a greater social good through the exchange and debate of ideas, is central to Appiah's assessment. 'Individuality is not so much a state to be achieved as a mode of life to be pursued', Appiah writes (EI: 5). Put differently, 'value' is found not simply in being 'different' (a status 'to be achieved') but in the ability for 'self-creation' ('a mode of life') (EI: 6). This dynamic of individual self-creation forms the basis of Mill's philosophy in *Utilitarianism* (1863), in which the ethical value of decision-making is predicated on what produces the most personal happiness for the greatest number of people. This approach, ideally, informs a person's 'plan of life', the dimensions and possibilities of which have since been contested. The tension between individual liberty and social equality, in particular, has been a source of contention, due to the fact that not everyone inherits or has access to the same 'plan of life'. How is equality possible given the variety of human conditions and their structurally imposed limitations? John Rawls's influential work *A Theory of Justice* (1971) is among the best-known treatments of this dilemma, examining the possibilities of 'distributive justice' as a means of reconciling personal freedom with social equality (Rawls 1971). As Appiah puts it in *The Honor Code* (2010), many people agree that 'equality' is important, but there remains the vexed question, 'equality of what?' (HC: 127). People can usually agree about what they are *against*, but they are not always in agreement about what they are *for*.

The uncertainty of equality leads Appiah to address the limits of individual freedom—what he calls 'the ethics of individuality'. An initial question is whether liberty can lead to arbitrariness. If we are responsible for our own choices and lives, this situation of free agency can lead to self-rationalization with little regard for others. It can lead to indulgence and solipsism—a life without consequence. A related problem is that individual liberty and autonomy can foster a lack of 'sociability' (EI: 15). Mill's definition of life as a commitment to 'one's self as a project' can permit such 'self-cultivation' to lead to disregard and conflict in social relationships. Appiah believes this situation can be avoided due to the interdependence of these two practices

(EI: 15, 17). Social relationships *assist* our self-cultivation. Yet, two other obstacles exist as well: a concern for authenticity and, differently, an existentialist view toward life. The first can diminish freedom by constraining behavior to a pre-existing set of social criteria. People of certain religious faiths or ethnic identities, for example, may be expected to comply with inherited cultural practices. The second imparts a sensibility that having a life plan and pursuing self-creation can be meaningless—a case of few cultural guidelines and perhaps too much freedom—thus curtailing agency. It turns out practicing individualism from an ethical or moral standpoint is not so easy.

Appiah further contextualizes these dilemmas of equality and freedom by making a distinction between personal and collective identities. Though personal freedom and self-creation are essential to making and affirming one's identity, collective identities can vitally inform and shape individual identities through pre-existing 'scripts' (EI: 22). As he writes, 'we should acknowledge how much our personal histories, the stories we tell of where we have been and where we are going, are constructed, like novels and movies, short stories and folktales, within narrative conventions' (EI: 22). Unsurprisingly, there can be tension between individual freedom and these scripts. Though people may have agency, these pre-existing scripts can be difficult to resist due to their social acceptance. It is easy to adopt an identity when that identity is publicly recognized and celebrated. On the other hand, these scripts can limit the freedom a person might have by reducing their options. Scripts that dictate gender norms under patriarchal conditions are a good example of this negative outcome. In sum, the concept of 'scripts' is helpful for understanding individual autonomy, while also demonstrating the uses of liberalism for literary analysis once more. As Appiah remarks, 'part of the function of our collective identities—of the whole repertory of them that a society makes available to its members—is to structure possible narratives of the individual self' (EI: 22). These scripts of collective identity can impart social, cultural, and political value. Collective identities can generate forms of solidarity and contribute to communal meaning (EI: 24, 25).

The matter of individual and collective identities also introduces the role of the state. Drawing from *On Liberty* and *Considerations on Representative Government* (1861), Appiah points to how Mill defined a 'good government' as a state that promoted 'the virtue and intelligence of the people themselves' (Mill as quoted by Appiah, EI: 26). To this end, states should provide education, alleviate poverty, and maintain infrastructure, among other measures, though the role of the state vis-à-vis individual freedom should ultimately be restricted. Individual liberty should reign. Isaiah Berlin (1909–97) proposed the idea of 'negative liberty'—a notion referring to preventing government intrusion in individual lives—as an elaboration of Mill's thinking. He also articulated the parallel term 'positive liberty' by which state support could aid people in achieving their aims (EI: 27). Affirmative action programs at schools and businesses are a good example of this kind of state intervention and assistance, which can enable 'the virtue and intelligence of the people' to flourish. This elusive equilibrium that Mill identified between state support for individuals and the notion of self-reliance therefore still endures.

'Autonomism' (not to be confused with autonomist Marxism) is a recent variation of Mill's individualism. This understanding of freedom is more abstract and extreme in Appiah's view, given that it references a form of absolute freedom without restriction. 'It has, indeed, become commonplace to stipulate that the autonomous agent has distanced himself from social influences and conventions', Appiah writes in describing this approach. The 'autonomous agent' in this instance 'conducts himself according to principles that he has himself ratified through critical reflection' (EI: 38). Yet, by extension, autonomism has been construed as promoting intolerance toward others in defiance of diversity. Mill and later liberal thinkers, such as the Indian economist Amartya Sen, have emphasized the importance of diversity in recognizing liberty and understanding equality (Sen 2009). The consequent issue at stake is how individualism, autonomist or not, can 'accommodate' diverse social groups and 'extend equal respect to their members' (EI: 43). Indeed, these social conditions are an essential 'precondition for the exercise of autonomy'

(EI: 43) since they not only shape how we treat others, but they also influence how others might treat us.

As Appiah summarizes, these issues have informed the tensions between proponents of liberal individualism and proponents of communitarianism (Sandel 1981; Tams 1998). The former expresses a continued belief in agency and autonomous self-creation while the latter recognizes social context and community, requiring limits to individuality and its self-directed choices of aspiration. An option of 'partial autonomy' or 'partial authorship' provides a compromise, though it implies the failure to achieve an ideal and leaves unclear the meaning of 'partial' (EI: 52). For Appiah, this debate over 'agency and structure' (EI: 56), which has equally preoccupied social scientists (Bourdieu 1977 [1972]; Giddens 1979), is ultimately one of emphasis, whether one is interested in the 'management of society' or 'individual liberty' (EI: 59). Furthermore, this debate often concerns not only 'what the world is like but what the world ought to be like' (EI: 59), which can leave consensus elusive. Before turning to solutions, however, it is necessary to address the structure of 'identity' itself.

THE STRUCTURE OF IDENTITY

Returning to his study of Du Bois in Berlin, Appiah highlights how much of Du Bois's work presaged present-day understandings of 'identity', a term whose current usage only gained acceptance during the 1950s and 1960s. It was not a category that Du Bois sought to conceptualize as such. Nonetheless, 'identity', with its elements of social recognition and self-fashioning, captures the dimensions of Du Bois's lifelong undertaking. As Appiah writes, in a manner that accords with classic liberalism, 'Du Bois certainly helps us see that the ethical significance of our identities derives from the way those identities give us projects' (LD: 159).

Appiah elaborates on the structural dimensions of 'identity' in *The Ethics of Identity*. 'Identity' of course pertains to individuals and groups alike, and it is essential to understand their interaction. Drawing on the work of the philosopher Ian Hacking,

Appiah provides one illustration of their interaction through the concept of 'social labels'. Social labels representing particular groups can inaugurate the person, a situation called 'dynamic nominalism' (EI: 65). For example, if a person is referred to as 'Ghanaian' or 'Korean' or 'American', that label immediately impacts that person. Indeed, the impact of such ordinary social labeling on individual freedom can run deeper and last longer than anticipated. 'Once labels are applied to people, ideas about people who fit the label come to have social and psychological effects', Appiah writes. 'In particular, these ideas shape the ways people conceive of themselves and their projects' (EI: 66).

Several additional points should be made. Identity labels must circulate and be acknowledged for identities to have meaning. Identities must be legible and definable to outsiders—those to whom the label does not apply—in addition to being recognizable and meaningful to whom the label does apply. This cognizance depends on pre-existing 'social conceptions' (EI: 67). These 'social conceptions' can also be understood more pejoratively as stereotypes. The content of these identities can therefore be subject to deliberation between outsiders and members of the identity group. The 'internalization' of labels is also important. As with 'scripts', Appiah cites the role of narrative as part of this process. 'By way of my identity I fit my life story into certain patterns', Appiah writes, 'and I also fit that story into larger stories ... Around the world, it matters to people that they can tell a story of their lives that meshes with larger narratives' (EI: 68). Concurrent to conforming to pre-existing narratives or scripts is the element of treatment once more. Narratives of identity can pre-determine and structure how other people view and behave toward people different from themselves.

In Appiah's view, these three elements of social conception, internalization and self-identification, and external treatment comprise a paradigm of identity for political and ethical life. This intersectional interpretation is vital in that it provides a multipart basis for 'people's shaping and evaluation of their own lives' (EI: 69). It can contribute to political life in the sense that acknowledging patterns of treatment can generate better understandings of how external factors of conduct can 'determine one's success and failure in living one's life' (EI: 69). Building on this latter point, there has been persistent debate as to the role of the state in such matters of treatment with 'reform liberalism' and 'egalitarian liberalism' submitted as remedies (Rawls 1971; Walzer 1983; Dworkin 2000).

Given the promotion of individual rights and freedom as a central tenet of liberalism, some view state acknowledgment of and assistance for social identities as *illiberal*. As Appiah summarizes, this vantage point believes such intervention conscripts the state into 'the business of advantaging and disadvantaging particular identities in ways that encroach upon the individual's freedom to shape his or her own life' (EI: 70). In contrast, multiculturalists believe 'the state *must* recognize these identities because without them individuals will lack what they need for making a life' (EI: 70). A middle position in this dispute accommodates social identities, but does not recognize them as such—an approach that approximates the argument for 'religious toleration' but not formal government recognition of religion, popularly known as the separation of church and state (EI: 71). Nonetheless, the question of state involvement remains crucial for understanding the uses and fate of 'identity'.

INDIVIDUAL RIGHTS, GROUP RIGHTS, AND THE MATTER OF PLURALISM

One way of navigating the question of social identities and the state is to address the issue of individual rights versus group rights. Appiah makes a distinction between 'ethical individualism' and 'substantive individualism', both of which are based on the classic liberal ideal of individual rights and agency discussed earlier. The difference is that 'substantive individualism' adheres to the belief that rights *only* apply to individuals, whereas 'ethical individualism' is less restrictive—individuals have rights, but groups may as well. Concurrent to this distinction, Appiah discusses 'collective rights' versus 'membership rights' (EI: 72). The difference in this instance is scale. The former regards social groups and their rights as a group—a nation of people expressing their right to self-determination, for example. The latter regards how individuals bear certain rights as members *within* particular groups. A member of a Native American community has certain rights because of their membership in that community, which would not pertain to non-members. Critics argue that state recognition of 'membership rights' can complicate accepted understandings of liberal individualism, given that such acknowledgment can convey the idea that some groups and their members have *more* rights than others.

However, Appiah believes that the flexibility of 'ethical individualism' can resolve such disputes. The expression and fulfillment of individual rights may or may not depend on the equivalent expression and fulfillment of group rights. 'If our selves are embedded in social forms [groups]—the most commonplace of communitarian commonplaces', Appiah writes, 'it might be impossible to treat individuals with equal respect without somehow coming to terms with those social forms' (EI: 73). On the other hand, he proposes that individual well-being may well depend on 'the flourishing of the identity groups within which the meaning of our lives takes its shape' (EI: 73). This 'homology' between persons and groups is common to many definitions of 'multiculturalism', and such 'flourishing' may once more require state intervention.

But trouble can arrive through what Appiah calls 'hard pluralism'. Though there is not universal consensus on its definition, it generally refers to how the rights of the individual are limited in favor of group rights. This privileging of group rights over individual rights has also been called 'millet multiculturalism'—an expression derived from the Ottoman Empire, where communities were recognized but the state did not interfere in their internal affairs. Millet multiculturalism places personal autonomy secondary to community interests. In sum, hard pluralism and millet multiculturalism both oppose substantive individualism, but they also present a problem for individual rights in relation to group rights, even under conditions that would appear acceptable and beneficial. For example, acknowledging Indigenous communities in the US and Canada and respecting their rights as groups can be positive. However, an approach of hard pluralism can offer little recourse to individuals seeking redress for mistreatment *within* the group. For example, a marital dispute involving gender violence may leave a woman without legal recourse beyond the community, despite the harm caused. Only the rights of the group matter, not those of its individual members.

A solution, Appiah submits, is 'soft pluralism' or 'liberal pluralism'. This approach favors the rights of individuals while also recognizing group rights. As Appiah comments, 'soft pluralists try to find a point of equilibrium between the rights of individuals and the integrity of intermediate associations [i.e., groups or communities]' (EI: 79). The term for this point of equilibrium is 'neutrality'. As suggested by the term itself, this intermediate proposition is difficult to agree upon and attain. Individuals typically have non-negotiable interests, as do groups. Laws are subject to interpretation. Achieving a 'neutrality of consequences' may therefore be impossible (EI: 82). However, the alternative idea of 'neutrality as equal respect' may provide a solution by acknowledging the *premise* of equivalence between sides, whether individuals or groups, if not an equivalence of outcome. This approach can potentially retain a liberal pluralism with substantive meaning (EI: 91).

This latter method often applies to situations that recognize the power of states to govern with a mandate that respects the interests of the popular majority without disregarding the interests of minority groups and individuals. For example, if the beliefs of a religious minority appear unreasonable or false to a religious majority, the interests of the religious minority should still be respected and tolerated. This guarantee of minority group rights is therefore similar to the religious freedom protected under the First Amendment of the US Constitution. However, the argument for 'neutrality as equal respect' can run into problems of definition. For example, how is 'religion' to be defined? Are there quantitative requirements, in terms of the number of believers, that make a set of beliefs tantamount to 'religion'? Or is definition purely qualitative through the substance and coherence of faith? This legal accommodation under the principle of liberal pluralism raises the question of 'identity' itself, which can be challenging to define given that 'identities are multiple and overlapping and context-sensitive, and some are relatively trivial or transient' (EI: 100).

Appiah notes a parallel approach to liberal pluralism by philosopher Charles Taylor referred to as 'the politics of recognition', which argues for the role of states as arbiters between identity groups (Taylor 1994). States can intervene to 'sustain identities that face the danger of self-contempt imposed by the social contempt of others' (EI: 101). This approach can be applied to situations involving racial minorities and the factor of racism. Indeed, as Taylor himself writes, 'the withholding of recognition can be a form of oppression' (Taylor 1994: 36). However, Appiah counters this logic to stress that 'the civil apparatus of such recognition' may 'ossify the identities that are their object' (EI: 110). For example, a refugee community that is officially acknowledged as a refugee community by law may have a difficult time moving beyond this status in the years ahead. Its members may achieve full citizenship, but remain outsiders and even pariahs at social and national levels. Appiah refers to this ossification as 'the Medusa Syndrome'—a situation where individual agency and self-making are once more constrained.

In sum, the role of state policy and intervention is conditional. State intervention can protect and sustain the rights of individuals and groups, but states can also be uninvolved, seek neutrality, or on occasion unintentionally invent problematic identities. What is important to grasp is Appiah's belief in the potential role of state intervention, but that this role be dependent on specific conditions—namely, that state involvement ultimately respects and ensures individual rights on an equitable basis. In keeping with the liberal tradition, Appiah does not propose a universal function or status for the state, but aims to raise awareness of its potential responsibilities and limits in addressing and managing identities.

CULTURAL RIGHTS AND CULTURAL PLURALISM

The question of cultural rights adds still more nuance to the debate between individual rights versus group rights. Culture can be a 'resource' for individuals to achieve their desired goals. The philosopher Will Kymlicka, for example, has argued that 'culture' provides 'the context of choice' for people to make their decisions. The matter of culture consequently 'accords with, rather than conflicts with, the liberal concern for our ability and freedom to judge the value of our life-plans' (Kymlicka as quoted by Appiah, EI: 121). Indeed, this argument shows how individual rights and cultural group rights can work together. The latter can contribute to the former, thus fulfilling the tenets of liberal individualism. As Appiah writes, 'Kymlicka believes that the conflict between individualism and group rights is a mirage ... It's no more illiberal for a society to protect my culture, in his view, than it is for a society to protect my property' (EI: 121–22).

For illustration, one case study that Kymlicka has examined concerns the rights of Aboriginal communities in Canada. He believes these communities should have certain 'cultural rights' in order to secure a context whereby Aboriginal individuals can suitably express their cultural agency to fulfill their personal life plans. He similarly promotes 'polyethnic' measures for recent immigrants to adjust to Canadian life. Such measures would recognize and support cultural practices so that immigrants, like Aboriginal peoples, would be able to fulfill their life plans (EI: 122). Yet, there are two unanswered questions for Appiah. The first regards how such polyethnic measures would be implemented—a paradox exists. On the one hand, the more members of a cultural group there are, the less need there is for additional state intervention to secure the protection of cultural practices. On the other hand, the fewer members there are, the more state measures might be needed. However, if there is a small number, is this use of state resources justifiable? The second question for Appiah regards the freedom to engage with and adapt to *other* cultures. Should not the agency of an Indigenous person or immigrant be respected if they seek to assimilate to Canadian culture? Cultural identity can too often be treated in an abstract way, with the possibility of multiple cultural affiliations being incompletely addressed.

PLANS OF LIFE IN AFRICAN LITERATURE

The idea of a 'plan of life' (or 'life plan') from John Stuart Mill is a concept that can readily be applied to works of fiction, verse, and drama. Indeed, individualism more generally can be readily transferred to characters in a narrative in order to frame and understand their personal motivations and constraints. To pick one example from African literature, Ngũgĩ wa Thiong'o's first novel *Weep Not, Child* (1964) is a coming-of-age story involving a boy named Njoroge, who is the first person in his family to attend a Western school. The time is late colonial Kenya, and Njoroge finds his life affected by the atmosphere of the Mau Mau movement and the independence struggle against the British through the political involvement of his father, Ngotho. Njoroge's 'life plan' of receiving an education and making his way to adulthood is therefore disrupted by the politics of the time. His sense of freedom is constrained by the events unfolding around him. This situation can be found in other classic African novels such as Cheikh Hamidou Kane's *Ambiguous Adventure* (*L'Aventure ambiguë*, 1962) and Tsitsi Dangarembga's *Nervous Conditions* (1988), each of which addresses the fortunes of a student who through schooling encounters both opportunity and dislocation — situations that require a revision of one's life plan in order to attain freedom and find personal fulfillment. In many instances in African fiction, the topos of 'tradition' and 'modernity' are what constrain and enable life plans to be fulfilled. In sum, the notion of 'life plans' demonstrates once more how elements of liberalism can be utilized as tools for literary analysis.

The question of cultural rights relates to another predicament: the 'preservationist ethic'. This expression refers to the 'perishability' of cultures and the need to preserve them (EI: 130). If certain kinds of group rights and individual agency depend on cultural context and cultural practices to sustain the freedom to pursue life plans, these elements must be preserved. Yet the scope of the preservationist ethic can become unclear beyond conspicuous cases of extreme violence and cultural extinction.

Cultural destruction can be a slow process occurring over generations, for example when immigrant families adapt to a new country. 'Assimilation is figured as annihilation', Appiah summarizes regarding this case study (EI: 130). However, assimilation to a new culture may afford the individual more rights and freedom than they would have otherwise. Similar to Kymlicka's polyethnic measures, the preservationist ethic erroneously views culture as static, which leads to the question of whether people or culture are truly benefitting from such preservation. As Appiah writes, 'it is far from clear that we can always honor such preservationist claims while respecting the autonomy of future individuals' (EI: 135).

Elaborating on this last point, Appiah notes that a troubling sense of affinity can emerge between 'culture' and 'race' among preservationists through the use of descent-based language. Citing an argument by the literary critic Walter Benn Michaels, Appiah writes that 'without some racialized conception of a group, one's culture could only be whatever it was that one actually practiced, and couldn't be lost or retrieved or preserved or betrayed' (EI: 137; Michaels 1995). Therefore, while preservation and cultural survival may appear morally correct on the surface, what concerns Appiah is how descent-based reasoning for defining 'culture' can constrain individual autonomy. For example, the logics of cultural preservation and cultural reproduction could limit the educational options of children, who are the future exponents of cultural identities. Orthodox religious communities are good illustrations of this scenario with children receiving spiritual instruction from a young age and into early adulthood, which can limit the possibility of other identities being pursued or taking hold. Furthermore, similar to race, culture may be construed not only through the need for preservation, but through a morally problematic dynamic of opposition—what Appiah refers to as 'negation as affirmation' (EI: 138).

There is an alternative. Rather than culture being understood as a 'resource' for individuals, it can be understood as a 'social good' for society at large. Culture is not 'a mere instrument' for individual use, to cite Charles Taylor (EI: 129). It can contribute to the pluralism of society as a whole. Appiah also extends his earlier arguments on race. He proposes the concepts of 'internal diversity' and 'external diversity' as a way of navigating the larger issue of 'cultural diversity'. The former fosters pluralism *within* communities while the latter encourages pluralism *among* communities. These concepts can come into conflict. External diversity can reinforce boundaries and definitions in a way that discourages and reduces internal diversity. For example, to recognize different national groups may encourage standards of definition that foster internal homogeneity and the silencing of internal differences on the basis of race, gender, or class. Yet internal diversity can also flourish and lead to the erosion of group cohesion, leaving only the shell of group identity. Internal diversity favors the individual, whereas external diversity favors the group. Appiah concludes that cultural 'diversity' and 'uniformity' of treatment must be valued together for the different sources of identity, security, and agency they offer. Diversity, both internal and external, can be conscripted into 'the service of individual well-being' (EI: 153). In the end, political liberalism and cultural pluralism are not incompatible, but neither is the tension between the two easily resolved.

SOUL MAKING

In the penultimate chapter of *The Ethics of Identity*, Appiah examines what he calls 'soul making', a term that draws on the Platonic notion of politics as 'the art of caring for souls', though it also hints at the influence of Du Bois once more (EI: 155). This discussion addresses Mill's argument that the success of a state depends on its ability to promote 'the virtue and intelligence of the people themselves' (Mill as quoted by Appiah; EI: 155). A more recent expression of this perspective is 'perfectionism': the idea that a government should 'promote the ethical flourishing of its citizens' (EI: 157). The notion of 'ethical flourishing' is of course subject to debate as touched upon earlier. Yet the overarching rationale is the idea that states should do more than simply provide and sustain the basic conditions to achieve present needs and ends. States, however involved or limited, should create and sustain a citizenry that insures the continuation of individual rights and liberty into the future.

The issue of soul making therefore revisits the question of what role governments should have in the lives of individuals. Negative liberals—the descriptor 'negative' coming from Berlin's notion of 'negative liberty' discussed previously—believe that 'there is a reasonable place for government in guaranteeing security of life and property and creating the framework of contract', but 'government should not interfere in the ethical dimensions of our lives, should not be guided by notions as to what lives are good and bad for a person to lead, once he or she has met the enforceable demands of moral duty' (EI: 158). Perfectionism, which encourages state involvement, is therefore seen as inviting state paternalism. A middle approach has focused on 'civic virtues', such as voting, which can contribute to political order, but not necessarily entail state intrusion into the ethical life of individuals. The main aim is to ensure the stability and reproduction of the state. However, such 'virtues' can be hard to determine or rationalize. Authoritarian regimes may have stable political orders through the inculcation of certain civic virtues, but is this morally justifiable? As Appiah writes, 'the distinction between aiming at the virtue of citizens for their own sake, on the one hand, and for the sake of the polity, on the other, can be hard to draw' (EI: 162).

Soul making for Appiah is defined as 'the project of intervening in the process of interpretation through which each citizen develops an identity—and doing so with the aim of increasing her chances of living an ethically successful life' (EI: 164). There are three areas for possible state intervention, including education, anti-discrimination law, and what Appiah refers to as correcting 'our defections from rationality' (EI: 165). Education is the clearest example of soul making, and anti-discrimination measures are a tool for ensuring individuals can exercise their own agency in pursuing education, employment, and personal happiness. They comprise forms of direct and indirect soul making, respectively. But 'defections from rationality' suggest a different order of concern related to an inability of individuals to make reasonable decisions. One example may be social media platforms today like Twitter and Facebook, which have enabled the spread of misinformation and conspiracy theories that have impaired the making of reasonable judgments for some people. Should these media platforms regulate their information, or does this constitute censorship? The expression 'defections from rationality' invites circumspection as to what conditions can lead to such situations, and whether such situations should present an opening for state intervention or not.

One provisional solution for Appiah is to ensure the availability of information and choice to attain ethical success. 'The ethical self I have spoken of requires that, in making our lives, we accumulate evidence, form beliefs, identify options for action, predict and evaluate their outcomes, and act', he writes. Yet, he goes on to observe, 'Ideals of rationality, as they are usually understood, involve both, so to speak, calculation and information—both instrumental and cognitive dimensions. In a variety of ways, we all fall short of these ideals' (EI: 170). One reason for this failure is that personal well-being is not always achieved by satisfying preferences—a stance promoted by 'utilitarianism'. Eating a tub of ice cream or buying a luxury car may satisfy us in the short term, but they may not contribute to our long-term health and happiness. 'Human irrationality', Appiah writes, 'is ubiquitous, and akrasia represents only a small subset of its varieties' (EI: 171). An alternative to avoid the eruption of irrationality is the notion of 'informed desire', which refers to having complete information before making a decision. But, as pointed to earlier, what if avoiding irrationality through further information is not enough? Or differently, what if bad ethical choices are made, not due to akrasia or ignorance, but because the identities involved are themselves irrational?

In response to the latter question, Appiah is particularly concerned about identities that are 'grounded in mystifications' (EI: 183), whether through inconsistency or by neglecting certain facts. Racial identity is an example of this kind of inconsistency. Many who embrace racial identity often do so to resist racism. Hard rationalists would see this identification that accepts difference and descent for some people only to reject it for others as erratic and unreasonable. It is unclear how states should attend to such inconsistencies. One possible answer is to maximize situations for freedom of expression and the right to association, thus minimizing recourse to identities that traffic in mystification or inconsistency. Antidiscrimination law is important in this regard, especially against the problem of stereotyping, which can normalize false beliefs and labels. Such stereotyping can limit autonomy. Education as soul making can also provide a remedy by enabling autonomy and promoting 'mutual knowledge across identities that is a condition for living productively together' (EI: 209). Overall, soul making can have a positive impact, despite autonomist fears. As Appiah writes, 'for identities that have, historically, been wrongly derogated, such soul making, however piecemeal, can be one of the duties of a state that cares equally for all its citizens' (EI: 198).

CONCLUSIONS

The Ethics of Identity concludes with a chapter on 'rooted cosmopolitanism', a concept that is more fully developed in the book *Cosmopolitanism* (2006), published only a year later and which will be examined in the next chapter. The liberal cosmopolitanism espoused by Appiah is his signature contribution to the liberal tradition. It is a key component of his 'postcolonial liberalism' mentioned before that is informed by his experiences in Ghana. Cosmopolitanism can be understood as an attempt at promoting liberal values and practices at a global level. Indeed, in terms of scale, one might compare his cosmopolitanism to the endeavor of Pan-Africanism supported by his father's generation in that it creates an identity—one political, cultural, and historical in scope—and a project, to use Mill's term, for those who share a politics that retains local roots but also embraces a worldliness and outlook extending beyond the nation-state. In this sense, rather than elevating Western liberalism above other political approaches, Appiah is revising the liberal tradition to meet global conditions as encountered today.

The Ethics of Identity resembles *In My Father's House* in its expansiveness, its polyphonic quality, as well as its interrogation of an unwieldy topic—liberalism, in this instance, rather than the African continent. Similar to his preceding work, he subjects the liberal tradition to critical assessment in search of a useful set of principles that are driven neither by nostalgia nor received doctrine, but instead by practical use in the present in order to reach ethically sound decisions and a fulfilling life. As Appiah summarizes, 'Actually existing liberalism, of almost any description, is more than a procedural value: it places a substantive weight on creating a social world in which we each can have a good chance at a life of our own' (EI: 211). Many of Appiah's positions subsequently involve 'some gesture toward a necessary equilibrium—between our bare and "informed" or "rational" preferences, between a concern for people as they are, and for people as they might be, the identities we have and those we might achieve' (EI: 212).

This goal of balance and the challenge of achieving it can be said to define life itself. And yet this conclusion should not lead to existential despair. An ethical life as defined by liberal values of autonomy, freedom, and self-creation can have value and meaning in spite of the uncertainties one might encounter. In defining an ethical life, Appiah suggests it should be measured by

> *both* the extent to which a person has created and experienced things—such as relationships, works of art, and institutions—that are objectively significant *and* the degree to which she has lived up to the projects she has set for herself (projects defined in part by way of her identifications).
>
> (his emphasis, EI: 162)

He summarizes that

> A life has gone well if a person has mostly done for others what she owed them (and is thus morally successful) and has succeeded in creating things of significance and in fulfilling her ambitions (and is thus ethically successful).
>
> (EI: 162–63)

A person's identity ultimately provides both opportunities and limits to helping others and to making individual meaning out of life.

5

COSMOPOLITANISM

Though often perceived as a buzzword referring to high fashion and elite travel destinations, cosmopolitanism in the world of political theory is an ethical practice, a way of being in the world. Liberal cosmopolitanism, as examined by Appiah, is designed to address pluralism on a global scale, beyond the nation-state, in contrast to the previous chapter's discussion. Indeed, it is important to grasp the contrarian nature of cosmopolitanism, given its disregard for conventional forms of political citizenship. As touched upon later in this chapter, cosmopolitan themes can be found in a number of recent novels that dwell on questions of citizenship and transnational belonging, including Chimamanda Ngozi Adichie's *Americanah* (2013) and Teju Cole's *Open City* (2011). In her recent book *The Cosmopolitan Tradition* (2019), Martha Nussbaum writes that cosmopolitanism 'need not involve politics: it is a moral ideal' (Nussbaum 2019: 3). But, as she and Appiah have noted, it has been linked to a set of political obligations, such as recognizing human rights and the issue of 'dignity'. Cosmopolitanism as a practice and ethos asks how we should treat other people, with identities different from our own, in other parts of the world. It also asks how we should see ourselves, our own identities, within a broader global context.

Appiah finishes *The Ethics of Identity* with an argument for 'rooted cosmopolitanism', an idea he elaborates further in *Cosmopolitanism* (2006). This idea and the parallel notion of 'cosmopolitan patriotism' can be seen as Appiah's signature contribution to the liberal tradition—a position that moves beyond autonomist versus communitarian debates to think more expansively beyond the nation-state. One can also see 'rooted cosmopolitanism' as a response to the Pan-Africanism of his father's generation. Not only does it intersect with his engagement with the ethics of liberalism discussed in the previous chapter, but it reflects the local diversity of the Ghana he grew up in—a counterpoint to the racial solidarities of the past—and the need to accommodate such pluralism of the past and present, locally and globally. 'Rooted cosmopolitanism' provides a means for negotiating these distinctions. As explored in this chapter, cosmopolitanism for Appiah is not only about looking outward upon the world, but also about the cultivation of one's individual identity to inhabit multiple worlds at once.

NATIVISM

In order to establish what 'cosmopolitanism' is, we might ask: What is its alternative? One answer touched upon already concerns conventional notions of citizenship tied to the nation-state and smaller political entities such as cities. Citizens of existing political communities can be cosmopolitan, but they are not required to be. Another answer, given the international dimensions of cosmopolitanism, is nativism—a notion that stresses indigeneity and cultural authenticity as the wellspring of identity and being. Nativism in its most malignant form is typically associated with xenophobic nationalism resulting in conflict and episodic violence. South Africa, Europe, and the United States, for example, have experienced this form of malevolent hatred in response to new immigrants and refugees since 2000.

Appiah's engagement with the long history of nativism provides a foundation for understanding why cosmopolitanism appeals to him. He has been interested in nativism primarily as a cultural formation. In Chapter 3 of *In My Father's House*, entitled 'Typologies of Nativism', Appiah examines the intersections between race, nation, and literature that emerged during the late 18th and 19th centuries, which fueled nativist ideology. To take an example from the early history of the United States, Thomas Jefferson's *Notes on the State of Virginia* (1785) connected race and culture through Anglo-Saxonism, which contributed to an emergent white nationalism that propelled settler-colonial expansion, resulting in the displacement and genocide of Native American states and communities from the East Coast to the Ohio River Valley and beyond (Belich 2009; Dunbar-Ortiz 2014). Language and literature substantiated this relationship between race and nation, replicating an argument first made by Johann Gottfried Herder, who was introduced in Chapter 3. Herder's 18th-century notion of *Sprachgeist* (spirit of language) has been influential for rationalizing connections between nation, culture, and race (see also Bhabha 1990). These connections between race, nation, and literature produced and reinforced a white nativist outlook that has remained in American culture to the present.

However, as Appiah points out, the issue of nativism is different for African writers and intellectuals. Drawing upon the argument of Benedict Anderson (1936–2015) from *Imagined Communities* (1983), Appiah contends that nationalism as an idea and political strategy was an outside discourse introduced by colonialism (see also Chatterjee 1986). Added to this complexity, many African writers worked in European languages, thus disrupting a key tenet of Herder. Appiah acknowledges the continued presence of local intellectuals, whether griots, imams, or other figures, but the vast majority of contemporary African literature is by Western-educated writers. 'Colonial education, in short, produced a generation immersed in the literature of the colonizers', Appiah writes, 'a literature that often reflected and transmitted the imperialist vision' (IMFH: 55).

Given the foreignness of nationalism and the continued use of European languages, this situation might appear poised to elude forms of nativism. Yet Appiah underscores how these inherited conditions have not been irreversible. 'The decolonized subject people write themselves, now, as the subject of a literature of their own', he stresses. 'The simple gesture of writing for and about oneself—there are fascinating parallels here with the history of African-American writing—has a profound political significance' (IMFH: 55). Postcolonial African writing has therefore embraced a Herder-like appreciation for Indigenous languages and values as sources of identity (e.g. Ngũgĩ 1986) and an attitude that European languages 'can be cleansed of the accompanying imperialist—and, more specifically, racist—modes of thought' (IMFH: 56). In response to this more optimistic reconciliation of Indigenous and European influences, Appiah has expressed concern for the latent nativist elements involved—namely, a structured 'typology' of 'inside and outside' (IMFH: 56). Though he denounces a Eurocentric 'universalism' along with a number of postcolonial critics (Chakrabarty 2000; Guha 2002; Cooper 2005), Appiah believes this reproach itself reproduces Herder's emphasis on Indigenous language, literature, and territory. Furthermore, many cultural 'traditions' deemed authentic may in fact be 'invented', with postcolonial nativism imitating or employing colonial constructions (Ranger 2012 [1983]). Appiah provocatively asserts, 'the course of cultural nationalism in Africa has been to make real the imaginary identities to which Europe has subjected us' (IMFH: 62). Nativism has consequently had paradoxical effects in postcolonial settings. 'Nativist nostalgia, in short, is largely fueled by that Western sentimentalism so familiar after Rousseau', Appiah remarks, 'few things ... are less native than nativism in its current forms' (IMFH: 60).

Some scholars have rebuked him on this point (Gyekye 1995; Oyĕwùmí 1997), though it must be stressed that Appiah is not against identification with local languages or social practices. Cultural detail in African writing can be self-validating. It can sustain the worthy ambition to create worlds irrelevant to 'European Others' but meaningful to African readers (Miller 1990). Of greater concern to Appiah is 'the multiplicity of the heritage of the modern African writer' (IMFH: 66). He concurs with Gayatri Chakravorty Spivak that the 'third-world intellectual' is 'a contradiction in terms precisely because ... intellectuals from the Third World are a product of the historical encounter with the West' (IMFH: 68). He urges that African writers and their work be contextualized, that contemporary literature be understood by 'seeing the writer, the reader, and the work in a cultural—and thus a historical, a political, and a social—setting' (IMFH: 71).

In sum, the problem with nativism is not only that it can tacitly embrace and redeploy 'the language of empire', but that it also 'ignores the reciprocal nature of power relations; it neglects the multiform varieties of individual and collective agency available to the African subject; and it diminishes both the achievements and the possibilities of African writing' (IMFH: 72). The postcolonial nativist orientation toward cultural conflict between Africa and the Euro-American West, which for Appiah amounts to '*the* topos of contemporary African literature' (his emphasis, IMFH: 72), can lead to distortions of African writing, with writers seeking to please non-African readers. Their work becomes 'ersatz exoticism, like the tourist trinkets in the Gifte Shoppes of Lagos and Nairobi' (IMFH: 72). Nativism can be a cul-de-sac that ignores history and, as a consequence, it can fail to fully confront the complex legacies of the past that inform the present.

Cosmopolitanism provides a different approach, a practice that recognizes a colonial past but also moves beyond such entanglements to engage with a global present. The British-American-Ghanaian-Nigerian writer Taiye Selasi has articulated a variation of this position and its possibilities in her popular essay 'Bye-Bye Babar' (2005), which promotes an ethos of 'Afropolitanism' in place of preceding ideas of what it means to be 'African' in the world (see also Mbembe 2007). Taken together, the arguments of Selasi and Appiah are principally about negotiating the present with an eye toward the future.

AFROPOLITANISM

The idea of 'Afropolitanism' first gained popularity with an online essay by the novelist Taiye Selasi entitled 'Bye-Bye Babar' (2005). The title refers to both the children's book series based on the character Babar the Elephant, as well as a line ('Hello, Babar') from the Eddie Murphy film *Coming to America* (1988), in which an African prince travels to Queens, New York. In her essay, Selasi describes how a new millennial generation has come of age, whose parents are from the African continent, but who have grown up in Britain, the United States, and other parts of the world. 'The whole scene speaks of the Cultural Hybrid', she writes, 'kente cloth worn over low-waisted jeans; "African Lady" over Ludacris bass lines; London meets Lagos meets Durban meets Dakar'. This cultural hybridity constitutes a new form of identity. 'They (read: we) are Afropolitans', she declares, 'the newest generation of African emigrants, coming soon or collected already at a law firm/chem lab/jazz lounge near you. You'll know us by our funny blend of London fashion, New York jargon, African ethics, and academic successes'. Selasi further explores this theme of 'Africans of the world' in her debut novel *Ghana Must Go* (2013), a story about a family whose scattered members come home to Ghana after the death of the family patriarch, Kweku Sai, whose passing leaves them to contemplate their different trajectories, the tensions between the past and present, and the layered meanings of 'home'. Afropolitanism is ultimately a critical position set against persistent stereotypes of African 'tradition' and localism. Though it has been criticized as an elite discourse (Coetzee 2017; Balakrishnan 2018), Selasi's intervention remains a touchstone for redefining 'African-ness' in the 21st century.

COSMOPOLITANISM

What responsibilities do we owe other people in other parts of the world, whom we will likely never meet? What moral concerns and individual ethics should guide this question of obligation? As indicated in the previous chapter, individual rights and the administration of policies affecting those rights are understood to inhabit distinct political communities. The liberal tradition has been defined by the relationship between states and individuals, anchored by the notion of the 'social contract' and its defining text, *The Social Contract* (1762), by Jean-Jacques Rousseau (1712–78). In principle, individuals freely enter into this relationship with states with the understanding that benefits, such as protection, education, and welfare, will result, enabling more individual freedom and self-creation. Therefore, should we care about others outside of our existing political community with its contractual relationships? And if so, how?

These questions have long preoccupied liberal philosophers. Adam Smith addressed it in *The Theory of Moral Sentiments* (1759), exploring the possibilities and limits of sympathy. Immanuel Kant believed in a single moral community at the global level. But rather than aspiring toward a single political community under some form of world government, he advocated a 'league of nations' as outlined in *Perpetual Peace* (1795)—an idea that would acquire institutional form in the 20th century. Cosmopolitanism is another part of this trajectory of liberal philosophy. Though associated and even used synonymously with such words as 'globalization' and 'multiculturalism' today, cosmopolitanism should be treated as a distinct term with its own genealogy. The word 'cosmopolitan' originated in the 4th century BC when Diogenes the Cynic (c. 404–323 BC) coined it to indicate a 'citizen of the world' (*kosmopolitês*) in contrast to ordinary citizens of the *polis* (city). In *The Cosmopolitan Tradition*, Nussbaum considers cosmopolitan identity as a radical gesture intended to upset norms of citizenship and social belonging, questioning the very purpose of ordinary political bonds (see also Feldman 2007). With its rejection of lineage and other inherited markers of identity, we might even see cosmopolitanism as a new and revolutionary form of humanism. Why, then, do we limit ourselves to some bonds and not others?

The idea of the social contract provides one answer. States can offer protection and welfare in a way that the world at large cannot. But if this is the case, why has cosmopolitanism endured? The invocation of global 'citizenship' in its definition offers one explanation, underscoring an alluring political potential for mobility and ultimate freedom. Beyond this attribute, it possesses two dimensions that appeal to the pre-existing concerns of Appiah and his work. First, cosmopolitanism recognizes difference in the world—the existence of varying identities, belief systems, and social practices that can work against universal assumptions and the political claims of local communities alike.

Second, given the global scale of cultural pluralism, cosmopolitanism provides a way of approaching and negotiating such pluralism from a moral standpoint by promoting the idea of obligation to other people, regardless of kinship or community. Cosmopolitanism is about reaching beyond the parameters of local political communities and their allegiances. The re-emergence of cosmopolitanism at the end of the last century can be explained on these grounds. It reflected the end of the Cold War, the rise of neoliberal globalization, and the concurrent intensification of political concern over multiculturalism in many democratic nation-states. As the anthropologist Arjun Appadurai has written, the stereotypes of the past, whether the ethnographer's isolated village or the singular identity of the citizen, have been obliterated by contemporary flows of information, capital, and people, if they ever existed at all (Appadurai 1996).

Yet these two aspects of cosmopolitanism are at times in conflict with one another. The universalization of obligation can clash with respect for social difference. As Appiah puts it, 'There's a sense in which cosmopolitanism is the name not of the solution but of the challenge' (COS: xv). Tensions can emerge that generate 'friction' (Tsing 2005) between loyalty to a community, such as a nation, and loyalty to humanity. This friction does not require a decision, nor is it necessarily bad. It can lead to an intermediate form of 'partial cosmopolitanism' (COS: xvii). As with his discussion of 'neutrality' described in the preceding chapter, Appiah advocates a measured negotiation of the seemingly inevitable contradictions resulting from efforts to reconcile local and global ties. 'Loyalties and local allegiances determine more than what we want', Appiah comments, 'they determine who we are' (COS: xviii). Cosmopolitanism, then, as a practice of allegiance is not meant to be 'some exalted attainment' (COS: xix). Rather, it speaks to essential 'habits of coexistence ... of living together, association' (COS: xix).

The diversity of Ghana, where Lebanese and Syrian residents intermingle with Ghanaian families, along with tourists from Greece, Hungary, and the British Isles, gives Appiah a reason for embracing cosmopolitanism (see also Quayson 2014). The image of Ghana he conjures is a contrast to the one imagined by nativists, Pan-Africanists, and many Europeans, among others. 'Cosmopolitanism is an adventure and an ideal', he writes with a flourish. It provides an alternative life plan for those, like him, who have multiple identities. But more than this, the escalation and naturalness of human migration and cultural interaction make a cosmopolitan ethos a foregone conclusion. 'Cosmopolitanism isn't hard work', Appiah stresses, 'repudiating it is' (COS: xx).

THE PROBLEM WITH CULTURAL RELATIVISM

The initial importance of cosmopolitanism for Appiah is that it provides a means of navigating social and political differences in the world. However, traveling to different parts of the world and engaging with cultures not our own does not guarantee a positive version of cosmopolitanism. Appiah uses the example of 19th-century British explorer Sir Richard Burton (1821–90), who traveled extensively in Asia, Africa, and the Middle East and was purportedly fluent in more than 25 languages, but who, nonetheless, still held disparaging perspectives toward many non-European peoples (COS: 11; Kennedy 2005: 23). Appiah emphasizes how lesser-known scholars and intellectuals have also embraced a 'cosmopolitan curiosity' while either sustaining a sense of Eurocentrism, as in the case of 'Orientalism' (Said 1978), or retaining an ethnographic distance and cultural non-judgment, which also goes against a cosmopolitan ethos of obligation.

While Appiah is critical of Orientalism and other Eurocentric structures of knowledge as discussed in Chapters 1, 2, and 3, he is also skeptical of cultural 'relativism'—the idea of respecting and maintaining cultural difference and impartiality, even when this stance is intended to be benevolent. Approaching the issue of relativism from a philosophical standpoint, he discusses how his difficulty with relativism can be defined by a distinction between 'facts' and 'values'. This understanding is rooted in a philosophical approach known as 'logical positivism', which he simplifies as 'Positivism' (COS: 17). Two different outlooks drive positivism: the first is conditioned by beliefs, and the second is shaped by desires. To explain these viewpoints, he paraphrases the argument of British philosopher Elizabeth Anscombe (1919–2001), in which 'beliefs are meant to fit the world' while 'the world is meant to fit desires' (COS: 18). Put simply, belief is limited to the world as we see it—what we see is what we believe. Desire, on the other hand, is about want—wanting the world to be *more* than what we see. Taken further, beliefs can be judged as accurate or inaccurate, whereas desires cannot be subjected to such verification, since they do not reflect the world as it is. The upshot is that sticking to the 'facts' is often safer and easier than entering the realm of 'desires' and the 'values' that motivate them. Positivists stick to the facts. Given that people from different places and societies tend to have different values and desires, positivists accept cultural differences based on fact, rather than considering or appealing to the desires and values of other people. Positivists favor 'relativism'.

We might therefore take positivism as common sense. Who doesn't approach the world on the basis of facts? However, this sense of confidence can contain inconsistencies. One problem with positivists is that they can depend too much on facts. On the one hand, if there is no evidence, a positivist will have no confidence or belief in what another person says. On the other hand, a positivist might overgeneralize on the basis of a limited set of facts and, moreover, a subjective interpretation of those facts. Indeed, Appiah ultimately unravels the positivist approach by noting that the interpretation of facts is typically based on 'values' that are shared. Concepts of 'good' and 'evil', for example, are socially determined and actively taught, passed down to the next generation through a 'language of values' (COS: 28). Stories, artwork, film, and other aesthetic mediums help convey this shared language of values. In short, this recognition of social and cultural context is counterposed against the claims of individualism and the subjective judgment of strict positivism. Facts are observed and interpreted through pre-existing belief systems. Positivism is therefore not a reliable way to approach cultural pluralism and the world at large, given that it claims objectivity while maintaining culturally situated biases. Furthermore, blinded by these inconsistent conditions, positivism may overlook common ground with other people that can lead to a cosmopolitan ethos.

THE PROBLEM WITH UNIVERSALISM, OR LIVING WITHOUT AGREEMENT

Situating facts and beliefs in time and social circumstances does not automatically lead to the disintegration of relativism. Indeed, the unreliability of facts can contribute to conflict rather than mutual understanding and connection. Appiah subsequently makes a distinction between 'thick' and 'thin' concepts, which he draws from political philosopher Michael Walzer (Walzer 1994). 'Thick' concepts refer to values that are multilayered and subject to local interpretation and debate. They are 'peculiar to particular societies' (COS: 47). Examples of such concepts are social taboos in different cultures regarding diet, marriage, and other everyday practices. 'Thin' concepts are values that are more abstract and universal. They are likely to be shared by communities across the globe. Examples can be attitudes about the immorality of murder or that a conflict between good and evil exists in the world. Thick concepts might be said to outnumber thin concepts. But thin concepts typically have a deeper essence, touching upon what it means to be human. Making this differentiation between thin and thick concepts is useful for securing understanding between different people and communities. Even if a person does not share or believe in a thick concept deeply held in another society, that person can acknowledge and understand the importance of that concept in that society. However, given that thick concepts can reinforce relativism, it is thin concepts that hold promise for closer dialogue and connection.

Appiah is careful not to slide into an argument for universalism in his discussion of thin concepts. 'Cosmopolitans suppose that all cultures have enough overlap in their vocabulary of values to begin a conversation', he writes. 'But they don't suppose, like some universalists, that we could all come to agreement if only we had the same vocabulary' (COS: 57). Using an expression of the Scottish philosopher W. B. Gallie (1912–98), Appiah argues that some concepts are 'essentially contestable'—that they are intrinsically subject to debate rather than consensus. Ideas of social justice or equality, for example, fall within the dictates of this expression. Disagreement can emerge about which elements deserve consideration and which are less essential. For example, social justice through affirmative action programs may be seen as a positive measure. But should such programs take into account the factor of race alone, or should elements of class and gender be considered as well? Such debates, while difficult and at times seemingly irresolvable, are not necessarily a problem according to Appiah. Rather, they demonstrate the elusiveness of universal agreement, a fact even when thin concepts, such as equality, are at play.

Universalism, therefore, poses a problem for the cosmopolitan thinker, though from a different vantage point compared to relativism. Relativism, while often respectful, is too detached, foreclosing any engagement on ethical grounds. Universalism, while suggestive of a single moral community in a Kantian fashion, can underestimate the effort required to achieve moral agreement, if moral agreement is even possible. Appiah summarizes three areas where disagreement can emerge over values. First, as noted, a shared 'vocabulary' of values may not exist (COS: 66). Second, even if a shared vocabulary for discussion and assessment of an issue exists, it can be subject to interpretation and fraught debate. Third, as an extension of interpretation and debate, different values can be important to different individuals. Since backpedaling to cultural relativism and its positivism is not an option, Appiah proposes an intermediate approach based on 'practice'. To live together, to debate together, and to be civil throughout are examples of such practices. 'Indeed, our political coexistence, as subjects or citizens, depends on being able to agree about practices while disagreeing about their justification', he writes (COS: 70). 'We can live together without agreeing on what the values are that make it good to live together', he continues, 'we can agree about what to do in most cases, without agreeing about why it is right' (COS: 71).

Appiah goes on to suggest that conflict between communities is often based on beliefs and principles that are intuitively grasped rather than consciously reasoned. If this element of intuition is recognized and understood as an effect of received behavior, it can become a step toward activating reason and, possibly, changing one's mind. This shift in thinking need not require complete agreement in values, only understanding.

'Understanding one another may be hard; it can certainly be interesting', Appiah summarizes. 'But it doesn't require that we come to agreement' (COS: 78). What is ultimately important for Appiah is an intermediate space for conversation. Such conversation does not entail consensus, only that 'people get used to one another' (COS: 85). Indeed, creating universal consensus is not the goal. Rather, Appiah supports an active and ethical notion of 'cosmopolitan curiosity' that enables discovery and the internalization of what is shared and not shared. 'We can learn from one another', he explains in defining this expression, 'or we can simply be intrigued by alternative ways of thinking, feeling, and acting' (COS: 97). Cosmopolitanism, in sum, is not synonymous with universalism, but an intermediate practice of engagement and discussion rather than harmony and accord.

IN PRAISE OF CONTAMINATION

Appiah raises two additional problems that have challenged the ethos of cosmopolitanism. The first is the ideal of 'preserving culture' and the second is the related accusation of 'cultural imperialism'. Preserving culture, as discussed in the previous chapter, can seem like a benign notion and practice, and one with relative ubiquity given the prevalence of museums, festivals, and other cultural institutions that collect and maintain traditions. But there are several problems that can arise. First, forms of tradition, whether dress, dance, or days of celebration, can be 'invented' (Hobsbawm et al. 2012 [1983]) and evolving, as Appiah noted in his discussion of nativism from *In My Father's House*. Claims of cultural authenticity are often on unstable ground, being that traditions can be far shallower historically than they appear on the surface. Similarly, Appiah believes that cultural imperialism is more subjective than statistically substantiated. Though popular commodities such as Coke and Hollywood films may indicate a dominant flow of goods and culture from the US to the rest of the world—a process of Americanization and homogenization more generally from center to periphery within a world capitalist system (Wallerstein 2004)—such views can overlook the resilience of local cultural practices and aesthetics, as well as the ways in which cultures from other parts of the world have influenced the US. Still, scholars have positioned counterarguments, highlighting the structural inequalities and violence of global capitalism that are obscured by 'cosmopolitanism' (Brennan 1997; Robbins 2017; Ramazani 2018: xxix). These competing characterizations can also ignore the role of individuals in negotiating these local and global worlds, a theme explored by the Nigerian writer Chimamanda Ngozi Adichie in her novel *Americanah* (2013).

CHIMAMANDA NGOZI ADICHIE AND *AMERICANAH* (2013)

Chimamanda Ngozi Adichie is a Nigerian novelist whose work has addressed the past and present of Nigeria through such novels as *Purple Hibiscus* (2003) and *Half of a Yellow Sun* (2006). She is also known for her polemic *We Should All Be Feminists* (2014) and her TED talk 'The Danger of a Single Story' (2009), which is critical of outside depictions of the African continent that have reduced it to singular narratives and images, whether portrayals of violence, poverty, or primitiveness. Her novel *Americanah* addresses the fates of two characters, Obinze and Ifemelu (Adichie's main protagonist), who begin dating while in secondary school in Lagos only to find themselves on separate life trajectories a short time later. Ifemelu leaves for the United States to study, confronting racism and what it means to be 'Black' in a way she had not before in Nigeria. Obinze attempts to follow her, but he is denied a visa to the US due to immigration restrictions after 9/11. He ends up in Britain, eventually becoming an undocumented immigrant. Through these plotlines, Adichie underscores the contingencies of mobility and globalization, especially the ways in which individuals confront pre-existing conditions, like racism or xenophobia, that can tragically diminish personal aspirations. Adichie's novel highlights the challenges of cosmopolitanism, which contrasts with Appiah's more sanguine view.

Beyond underlining the inconsistencies of cultural preservation and cultural imperialism, Appiah proposes a counterargument that he calls 'contamination'. He borrows this term from the Roman playwright Terence, whose full name was Publius Terentius Afer (c. 195/185 BC–c. 159 BC). Terence was born in Carthage in North Africa and later enslaved and brought to Rome. Despite such inauspicious beginnings, he was acclaimed in his lifetime for adapting Greek plays into Roman versions— a process of revision that critics referred to as 'contamination' (COS: 111). Terence is best known for the aphorism: 'I am human: nothing human is alien to me' (COS: 111). Appiah embraces this remark as the credo for his own view of cosmopolitanism and cosmopolitan curiosity. But what is more important is how the term 'contamination' captures the dynamic nature of culture, which in his view is incorporative, changing, and polyphonic. In his words, 'Cultural purity is an oxymoron' (COS: 113). 'Contamination' can be compared to other concepts such as 'creolization' and 'entanglement' (Glissant 1990; Thomas 1991). Édouard Glissant (1928–2011) is particularly useful to think with alongside Appiah. He and other Martinican intellectuals, such as the novelist Patrick Chamoiseau, formulated the notion of *créolité* (creole-ness) as a counterpoint to Négritude by stressing the cultural pluralism of the Caribbean rather than a unitary humanism based on racial identity. In these ways, cosmopolitanism is part of a broader repertoire of cultural theory that emerged during the postcolonial period and after.

ÉDOUARD GLISSANT AND *CRÉOLITÉ*

Édouard Glissant (1928–2011) was a novelist, poet, and critic from the island of Martinique. He was a contemporary of Frantz Fanon and, like Fanon, a former student of Aimé Césaire, a founder of the Négritude movement. Responding to the previous generation, Glissant established a new set of ideas and positions intended to critique Négritude and its parameters. One tactic was to assert *Antillanité* or 'Caribbean-ness' as a distinctive regional identity and cultural formation, in contrast to the transatlantic

Pan-Africanism of Négritude. This emphasis was designed to work against the monolithic definition of Blackness upheld by Négritude. It also accommodated the racial and cultural diversity—Indigenous, Black, white, South Asian, Chinese, mestizo—within the Caribbean. In a move resembling cosmopolitan curiosity, his concept of *détour* ('diversion') argued that self-knowledge could come through engagement with other peoples and cultures. His major works include *Caribbean Discourse* (1981) and *Poetics of Relation* (1990). His critical stance toward Négritude and embrace of *Antillanité* inspired a generation of writers and intellectuals, among them Patrick Chamoiseau, Jean Bernabé, and Raphaël Confiant, who co-authored the manifesto *In Praise of Creoleness* (1993).

Yet these intergroup aspects of culture have not stymied arguments for control and ownership. Appiah discusses in *Cosmopolitanism* the notion of 'cultural patrimony', sanctioned and pursued in part by different UNESCO efforts, whereby cultural creations are seen to reflect particular societies and as a consequence are understood to be the heritage and property of groups as opposed to individuals. This situation has raised questions of authorship and ownership rights for the individual artist, though it has primarily generated controversy over museum collections that accumulated artwork and artifacts through colonial conquest. Appiah parses the different dimensions of this divisive topic, pointing out how works of art and other items of heritage possess elements from different cultures—there is no 'pure' heritage—while also denouncing how attention has focused on the return of objects to their original homes without full consideration of the expense and ethical implications involved. Such acts of physical return can assist local senses of self-identification and cultural pride, but the pursuit of restitution can neglect opportunities to cultivate a cosmopolitan sensibility in place of an imperial one. In this way, a type of postcolonial cultural relativism can result. Appiah further notes that claims of 'cultural patrimony' have been extended through new legal guidelines of 'intellectual property', which have included a wider range of intangible artifacts, beyond material objects, such as cultural ideas, stories, and practices in the past, present, and potentially the future (COS: 128). The origin myth of a Native American community, for example, might be licensed as intellectual property for the protection—or sale—of that story. This licensing approach comes from Euro-American notions of property rights, and, given the lucrative prospects at hand, such legal moves toward Indigenous cultures resemble those made by corporations such as Disney toward their cultural creations (COS: 130).

Ultimately, control over cultural heritage is more fraught than it might appear on the surface. The potential for inaccurate cultural definitions, disregard for individual artists, and stringent intellectual property rights, which reflect what legal scholar Lawrence Lessig has called 'property fundamentalism', comprise key parts of this complexity (COS: 130). Ongoing expense is another matter, both in terms of returning items and preserving those items once they have been repatriated, especially in countries that may not have the infrastructure or personnel to maintain them. Nonetheless, there are valid reasons for return, including 'site-specific' aesthetic rationales, purposes of religious practice or ritual, and, of course, in cases of documented theft (COS: 132). In short, there are strong justifications for both pursuing return as well as questioning it. What concerns Appiah the most is that debates over cultural patrimony can marginalize a cosmopolitan ethos in which connections can be made 'not *through* identity but *despite* difference' (his emphasis, COS: 135). In his view, cultural patrimony can stop dialogue, reinforce cultural relativism, and thus prevent the possibility of a cosmopolitan worldview from taking hold.

COUNTER-COSMOPOLITANISM AND MORAL OBLIGATION

Against this backdrop of pervasive relativism, how, then, does a sense of obligation for others across difference and distance arise? One answer is to consider the fact of already existing transnational communities, which can bind people together across the globe. Such cultural and diasporic communities can be a benevolent force, though this affirmative outcome is not always guaranteed. Appiah expresses anxiety for what he terms 'counter-cosmopolitans'. In this instance, his thoughts regard fundamentalisms of different global faiths, whether Christian, Muslim, or Jewish, that promote a 'universalism without toleration' (COS: 140). By this idea, he means how these different faiths stretch across geographies, defying the nation-state and other forms of community, in a way that can approach universality. This sense of universalism is reinforced through a cohesive worldview that fosters commitment to a certain set of beliefs. As a consequence, these forms of universalism can have positive effects by providing moral guidance, social dictates, and producing communities of belonging more generally. However, even when these forms of universalism are not malignant, they still form a point of contrast to cosmopolitanism on grounds of pluralism and 'fallibilism' (uncertainty of belief) (COS: 144). 'Cosmopolitans think that there are many values worth living by and that you cannot live by all of them', Appiah writes with regard to the first term. 'So we hope and expect that different people and different societies will embody different values' (COS: 144). With regard to the latter term, he comments that cosmopolitans assume that 'our knowledge is imperfect, provisional, subject to revision in the face of new evidence' (COS: 144). The trouble with religious faith is that it tends to be intolerant toward pluralism, at least religious pluralism, and it typically retains a doctrinaire self-righteousness that is hardly conducive to the cosmopolitan desire for debate and exchange.

In contrast to these 'counter-cosmopolitanisms' are cases of moral apathy—another dilemma. If cosmopolitanism is, as Appiah quips, 'universality plus difference', there is the competing problem of those who reject the uses of universality on any basis (COS: 151). This lack of belief is not necessarily predicated on ignorance or a limited worldview. It is defined by simple inaction. 'The real challenge to cosmopolitanism isn't the belief that other people don't matter at all', Appiah comments, 'it's the belief that they don't matter very much' (COS: 153). The principal question, then, is what we owe strangers, whether we encounter them on a firsthand basis or not. He cites Adam Smith's book *The Theory of Moral Sentiments*, mentioned earlier, in which the moral question of obligation is raised by comparing one's own immediate bodily pain to a disastrous earthquake in China affecting thousands of people, thousands of miles away. Which situation should inspire moral concern and response? It is easier to focus on and address one's own problems, but the sheer level of human tragedy in China, however distant, is far greater. A pragmatic approach to this dilemma is to agree that we cannot expect to have the same sense of feeling for distant strangers as we do toward ourselves and our intimate acquaintances. But is this morally justified?

Smith's scenario is not unique: variations of his analogy continue to be invented by present-day philosophers. Furthermore, specific to the question of cosmopolitan ethics, which promotes concern for people elsewhere, the world has become much smaller given that travel and communication are far easier than they were in Smith's time. Appiah cites a scenario by the Princeton philosopher Peter Singer, in which a child is seen drowning in a pond. Should one save the child, regardless of any inconvenience or discomfort this rescue might cause to the person doing the saving? The immediate answer is yes. The 'Singer principle' therefore 'requires you to prevent bad things from happening if the cost is something less awful' (COS: 160). However, though there is an obvious moral rationale to this perspective—saving a person's life—it also raises the question of limits, especially when the scale is greater. Should a country intervene in the affairs of another country in order to prevent genocide? This decision can be harder to reach, even with advanced signals and information, as in the failure of the international community to prevent the genocide in Rwanda in 1994. Questions of 'humanitarian intervention' have since been debated. As with Smith, the question of 'distance', geographic and otherwise, is raised once more. Rather than having intimate knowledge or not about the potential victim, the question is often reframed to ask whether there is less 'cost'—in terms of time, money, and energy—in helping those who are near, rather than those in need who are far away. For many, local commitments are easier to fulfill. But does this imperative of helping locally contribute to a global moral good? Does it not erode the adapted sense of universalism pursued by cosmopolitanism?

In response to these questions, Appiah says the cosmopolitanism he supports 'prizes a variety of political arrangements' (COS: 163), thus alleviating the ethical burdens that Adam Smith's query and the Singer principle place on individuals. The nation-state in particular is positioned as the 'primary mechanism' for ensuring that global needs and obligations are met. By extension, such needs and obligations should be shared across the international community; they should not be construed as the responsibility of an individual nation. However, Appiah also believes that it is natural to feel a greater sense of responsibility and affinity to those closer to us. 'Whatever my basic obligations are to the poor far away', Appiah writes, 'they cannot be enough, I believe, to trump my concerns for my family, my friends, my country; nor can an argument that every life matters require me to be indifferent to the fact that one of those lives is mine' (COS: 165).

Appiah consequently proposes an intermediate approach similar to his appraisal and advocacy of neutrality vis-à-vis liberalism discussed in the preceding chapter. Action as a matter of practice and circumstance will often be local. Yet this view does not mean one should be morally non-committal to situations elsewhere. 'Cosmopolitanism is about intelligence and curiosity as well as engagement', Appiah writes (COS: 168). Furthermore, following Smith's early example, Appiah argues that what is needed is 'the exercise of reason, not just explosions of feeling' (COS: 170). 'Faced with impossible demands, we are likely to throw up our hands in horror', Appiah remarks. 'But the obligations we have are not monstrous or unreasonable. They do not require us to abandon our own lives' (COS: 173). In this sense, a balanced commitment must be struck between attending to our local responsibilities and recognizing that our moral obligations extend beyond our immediate surroundings as well.

ROOTED COSMOPOLITANISM AND THE LIBERAL PROJECT

The idea of 'rooted cosmopolitanism' or 'cosmopolitan patriotism' is an attempt by Appiah at capturing this intermediate version of cosmopolitanism, one that aspires toward universal attention and engagement while also legitimating an inclined partiality toward local concerns. These expressions possess intentional surface paradoxes. The first term is partly an appropriation and positive revision of an anti-Semitic epithet about Jews being 'rootless cosmopolitans' (EI: 329 n.10). The second term derives from the experience and worldview of his father, Joe Appiah, who 'never saw a conflict between his cosmopolitan credo and the patriotism that quickened his spirit and defined his largest ambitions' (EI: 223). As the younger Appiah explains in his earlier essay 'Cosmopolitan Patriots' (1997),

> the cosmopolitan patriot can entertain the possibility of a world in which *everyone* is a rooted cosmopolitan, attached to a home of one's own, with its own cultural particularities, but taking pleasure from the presence of other, different places that are home to other, different people.
>
> (his emphasis, Appiah 1997: 618)

What is at stake, however, for liberal thinkers on this matter of mutual obligations is a pre-existing tension between three concurrent dimensions: securing individual autonomy and freedom; promoting civic loyalty and associational life; and practicing moral equality and fair treatment. How can such central principles of liberalism contribute to cosmopolitanism as a moral philosophy?

As mentioned briefly before, *The Ethics of Identity* addresses cosmopolitanism in its final chapter, titled 'Rooted Cosmopolitanism'. This chapter is a pivot point between *The Ethics of Identity* and *Cosmopolitanism*, at once summarizing the first and presaging the next. For *The Ethics of Identity*, it provides a signature moment for Appiah to depart from his liberal predecessors by moving beyond the Euro-American context to think globally about the potential of liberalism in the world.

Appiah is not alone, having been preceded by John Stuart Mill and his problematic imperial outlook, which allowed for the possibility of individual rights for the colonized in the future. More recently, the Indian economist and philosopher Amartya Sen has made contributions to the liberal tradition through the idea of 'development as freedom' (Sen 1999). Yet Appiah's embrace of cosmopolitanism can be seen specifically as a critical departure from Mill, given that Mill's comments on colonial subjects were not only disparaging but also antithetical to a cosmopolitan ethos. For Appiah, rooted cosmopolitanism provides a means for balancing membership in local political communities, such as nation-states, while maintaining a concern for people outside of those communities. He expresses disdain once more for 'toxic cosmopolitans', such as religious fundamentalists, whose counter-cosmopolitan approach can be both 'staunchly supranational and also staunchly illiberal' (EI: 220). Yet he also recognizes that an unmodified or 'extreme' cosmopolitanism is also difficult to embrace, given the importance of local relationships once more and the stronger bonds and feeling that they may impart.

In explaining 'rooted cosmopolitanism', Appiah adheres to the distinction between 'ethics', which inform and regulate personal decisions, and 'morality', which relates to how we treat other people. This difference is further amplified through his understandings of 'thick' and 'thin' concepts discussed earlier. 'Moral obligations must discipline ethical ones', Appiah writes. 'Yet this is not to say that the obligations of universal morality must *always* get priority to ethical obligations—to others or to ourselves' (his emphasis, EI: 233). He advocates the reasonableness of partiality toward those with whom we have 'thick' social ties. Forms of identification can create ethical communities that matter more to us than others. Citing a perspective by Nussbaum (1994), Appiah concedes that primary attention to local circumstances may in fact be the best way to promote moral good (EI: 240).

By extension, Appiah advocates the role of intermediate institutions—the governments of nation-states, for example, as touched upon earlier—for promoting and arbitrating the moral tasks of liberal cosmopolitanism. One way of navigating competing tendencies toward universalism and anti-universalism is through mediated conversation between such political entities, the issue of human rights being a good example. He cites the phrasing of the human rights scholar Michael Ignatieff in particular, that human rights have 'gone global by going local' (EI: 260). Put differently, human rights cannot be universally acknowledged or adhered to by proclamation alone. Local efforts are needed, and compliance is a constant challenge. One discussed technique is to regard human rights as 'side-constraints', a term of philosopher Robert Nozick (1938–2002), in which universal human rights can mark boundaries that acknowledge locally meaningful individual rights without sacrificing the uses or impact of universal human rights (Nozick 1974). The two sets of rights work in conjunction.

Appiah is thus in favor of limiting the language and uncritical application of human rights. 'All I am insisting is that not every good needs to be explained in the language of human rights', he remarks, 'a language that makes most sense if it is kept within bounds' (EI: 263). He prefers that human rights be 'a language for deliberation, or argument, or some other form of conversation' (EI: 264). To be clear, Appiah is not *against* human rights. However, in his view, human rights have gained traction around the world because they relate to many metaphysical understandings of personhood and well-being already accepted within local and regional communities. He cites the Akan concept of *animuonyam* (respect) as an example of such pre-existing ideas. These moral vocabularies contribute once more to Appiah's version of liberal cosmopolitanism, which situates pluralism as enabling individuals to achieve their aims. In his words, the 'cosmopolitan impulse' views 'a world of cultural and social variety as a precondition for the self-creation that is at the heart of a meaningful human life' (EI: 268).

CONCLUSIONS

In his novel *Open City* (2011), the Nigerian-American writer Teju Cole briefly mentions sending a copy of Appiah's *Cosmopolitanism* to an acquaintance. Indeed, this novel explores a number of themes found in Appiah's work with its meditations on identity, culture, and the habitation between worlds (Sollors 2018), with Cole's narrator, Julius, a young psychiatrist, navigating emotions, ideas, and the city of New York during the early 21st century. The plot itself, with its elements of wandering and observation, imparts a philosophical approach to everyday circumstances, and it underscores the role of personal autonomy in enabling such freedom of mind. It is a good example of how liberal ideals can be used to write and interpret literary fiction. The internal monologue of Julius and his engagements with the world exhibit a cosmopolitan curiosity and the possibilities of having such an ethos without constant travel—a mistaken assumption often made. And yet the stark ending of the novel also demonstrates that possessing a cosmopolitan attitude does not guarantee ethical behavior. The revelation that Julius sexually assaulted his childhood friend, Moji, forces the reader to revise their accumulated understanding of him. His worldliness comes across as shallow and his life as a facade. As Appiah addresses in the concluding paragraphs to *The Ethics of Identity*, 'Cosmopolitanism values human variety for what it makes possible for human agency' (EI: 268). Yet the effects of this agency may not always be positive. Bruce Robbins, a noted critic of cosmopolitanism, has argued that this ethic has encouraged 'humanitarian' gestures without full accountability—those in the West who seek to help the impoverished elsewhere in the world neglect their direct or indirect responsibility in creating these conditions of want (Robbins 2017). The remaining question, then, is how such individual agency and variety of human experience can contribute to progressive change in the world. The next chapter provides a tentative answer by examining Appiah's book *The Honor Code* (2010).

6

MORAL REVOLUTIONS

If the preceding chapters have a unifying conclusion to offer, it is that, for Appiah, the person precedes the group, and ethics precede politics. Here the difference between ethics and morals reveals his steady concentration on the individual: ethics concern individuals and morals concern society. Furthermore, race, culture, and other social identities do not always play a positive role in individual lives or society in that they can constrain agency and often have fictional attributes, if not always being entirely fictional in their effects. In line with the core principles of liberalism, Appiah believes that agency and self-creation give life meaning, not identities by themselves. Cosmopolitanism, Appiah's preferred approach to being in the world, marks a global extension of the liberal tradition. Liberalism and cosmopolitanism are not only compatible, but the latter can be seen as a grander magnification of the former. As he elaborates at one point, 'Cosmopolitans do not ask other people to maintain the diversity of the species at the price of their individual autonomy' (EI: 268). Overall, Appiah's concerns for how to live ethically and, thus, how to live well fall within the parameters of liberal philosophy.

This emphasis on the individual and personal freedom leaves open the question of how to achieve broader social change. If liberalism is only concerned with the happiness of individuals, why care about the happiness of others? It may appear that liberalism and revolutionary change at a societal level are incompatible, even though both aspire to self-determination, but on a different scale. As discussed in Chapters 1 and 4, one way to understand the appeal of liberalism for Appiah is generational. Having grown up amidst decolonization and its forms of revolutionary change, Appiah indicates what liberalism can look like from the vantage point of Africa. More specifically, while discussing the political career of his father at the end of *The Ethics of Identity*, Appiah provides an answer as to how the rights of the individual became of primary importance to him. 'Two things, in particular, strike me about the local character of the source of my father's increasing commitment to individual rights', Appiah reflects, 'first, that it grew out of experience of illiberal government; second, that it depended on a sense of his own dignity and the dignity of his fellow citizens that was the product of Asante conceptions' (EI: 269). The illiberalism he mentions was a feature of both colonial and postcolonial states. The postcolonial liberalism Appiah espouses is therefore a response to the forms of autocracy he and his father witnessed in Ghana, which also characterized many other newly independent countries. Postcolonial liberalism is an approach designed to ensure political expression and individual rights and autonomy by drawing on local and introduced notions of rights alike. But this position still raises the problem of how broader political transformation is possible. Are other forms of revolution possible apart from that espoused by Nkrumah and other leaders of the era of decolonization? *The Honor Code* (2010) provides one answer through its examination of 'moral revolutions' and their consequences.

RESPECT AND HONOR

Appiah defines 'revolution' as 'a large change in a short time' with 'moral revolution' involving a change in 'moral *behavior*' (his emphasis), instead of solely attitudes or perspective (HC: xi). Moral revolutions differ from the revolutions we are accustomed to reading about, those that involve popular rebellion, the overthrow of states, and the establishment of new political orders. The moral revolutions he examines include the end of dueling, footbinding, and slavery, and he notes that the moral arguments and views that led to such changes were well established before any actual change took hold. In short, there is a disjuncture between thought and expression, cause and effect, and morality and politics.

Accompanying this dynamic of moral revolution are social understandings of honor, shame, and their relationship to identity. These concepts can either instigate or prevent moral revolutions from happening. Citing the influence of Hegel and his term *Anerkennung* (recognition), Appiah stresses that concern for public respect and status motivates the shift from private moral sentiments to public moral behavior. At the level of the individual, there is a human need for recognition. But more than this basic desire, people want to be seen in ways that avoid shame and garner respect. Put differently, in contrast to the discussions of the preceding chapters, identities are not simply about social categories of identification such as race, culture, nation, or religion, but they can also be about moral perception. The individual desires to be seen as an ethical person in the public eye. Naturally, we want to be identified with qualities of admiration and integrity rather than disgrace or avarice. In addition, Appiah notes that identifying with and seeking to achieve honor can contribute to personal happiness and well-being. Appiah uses the Aristotelian term *eudaimonia* (flourishing), a word often translated as 'happiness', to capture this aim of honor. 'One way to begin to grasp why honor matters to ethics is to recognize the connections between honor and respect', Appiah writes, 'for respect and self-respect are clearly central human goods, too, things that add to *eudaimonia*, helping us to live well' (HC: xv).

Despite its centrality to social relations, modern philosophy has nonetheless neglected honor in Appiah's appraisal. It amounts to a vital theme, since 'like our social identities, it connects our lives together' (HC: xv). But more than social connection and personal recognition, honor when pursued in a sustained, critical fashion can contribute to social change and possibly moral revolutions. As he writes,

> One day, people will find themselves thinking not just that an old practice was wrong and a new one right but that there was something shameful in the old ways. In the course of transition, many will change what they do because they are shamed out of an old way of doing things. So it is perhaps not too much to hope that if we can find the proper place for honor now, we can make the world better.
>
> (HC: xvii)

The case of dueling is a good example of how personal honor can perpetuate an *immoral* practice, and how such practices can gradually lose their original connotations of honor and respect as a result. As Appiah underscores, this perception of immorality developed before the practice itself was banned, leaving open the possibility of a moral revolution. To end an immoral practice therefore requires more than a collective agreement that a behavior is wrong. It necessitates a shift in public attitude about how respect is earned and how dignity is upheld.

Appiah focuses on an episode in March 1829, when the Duke of Wellington (Arthur Wellesley, 1769–1852), prime minister of the United Kingdom, engaged in a duel with the Earl of Winchilsea (George Finch-Hatton, 1791–1858), who had accused him of 'plotting an assault on the Protestant constitution' (HC: 8). Wellington had supported the Catholic Relief Act of 1829, which would allow Catholics to be elected to the British Parliament. It was a matter of importance for Ireland, then under British rule, and Wellington's promotion of the act was to ward off Irish dissent. Beyond the specifics of this political dispute, however, was the personal honor of Wellington. Winchilsea's public accusation against Wellington, who was a hero of the Battle of Waterloo (1815), and his political actions constituted an *ad hominem* attack on Wellington's honor. Only a duel with pistols could resolve this indignity.

As Appiah points out, this means of conflict resolution went against Christian morals, civil law during that period, and Wellington's own conscience. Nonetheless, given the nature of honor at the time, Wellington had no choice but to go beyond the political dispute at hand to address the charge against his integrity. It is at this point where distinguishing the concepts of 'respect' and 'honor' is important. Appiah describes 'respect' as being about how others judge us, while 'honor' is about how we judge ourselves. To address the first, he draws out two additional notions of 'respect'—the idea of 'appraisal respect' versus the idea of 'recognition respect'—derived from philosopher Stephen Darwall (HC: 13). 'Appraisal respect' involves the measurement of respect due to a person through an external standard. For example, a person may garner public respect for the number of books they have published or for the number of professional tennis matches they have won, each of which demonstrates a level of commitment and excellence at a certain skill. 'Recognition respect' has less to do with achievement and more to do with the individual qualities of a person. For example, a person might be publicly acknowledged for a unique skill or talent that is hard to measure, or celebrated for a special achievement no one has attained previously. The accomplishments of Helen Keller (1880–1968), despite her disabilities of hearing and vision, could fall into this category, or the success of Toni Morrison as the first African American to receive the Nobel Prize in Literature. But 'recognition respect' can also be more ordinary. Appiah points out that someone may be granted 'recognition respect' for having a medical condition or a similar limitation. In this case, respect is not about accomplishment or power, but about deserving sympathetic or empathetic treatment.

These two notions of respect, which for Appiah also correspond to 'esteem' (appraisal respect) and 'positive regard' (recognition respect), relate to two notions of honor (HC: 13–14). In the first case, esteem is an effect of 'competitive honor': we earn the esteem of others through the honor we gain through competition. In the second case, positive regard is an effect of 'peer honor': we earn this recognition through social interaction and by demonstrating our ethical selves through such interaction (HC: 14). Though honor is typically self-driven as noted before—we do things as a matter of personal honor—it is important to recognize that notions of honor are typically pre-established through 'honor codes', rules of behavior that are socially defined and inherited. These codes are tied to the cultures we are born into. A brief example can be drawn with Okonkwo, the main protagonist of Chinua Achebe's acclaimed novel *Things Fall Apart* (1958). Okonkwo's stature and public respect are based on his skills as a wrestler and the honor he gains from this reputation. However, his circumstances of competitive honor and peer honor radically change by the end of the novel with the arrival of the British—a point that will be revisited. What is important here is how personal honor and the honor codes from which they derive are socially constructed. They are not permanent but subject to change and transformation.

These distinctions between 'respect' and 'honor' shape the behavior of people. Public respect, and fear of disrespect, can be a motivating factor for decision-making. The internal dynamic of honor is slightly different. Honor, for example, can dictate decision making to achieve this principle in and of itself, rather than any public recognition or material compensation. 'For the honorable person, honor itself is the thing that matters, not honor's rewards', Appiah writes. But other feelings—'shame' and 'pride' in particular—also exist and can shape honor's meaning. Shame arises 'when you have not met the standards of the honor code; and you feel it … whether or not anyone else knows you have failed' (HC: 16). This self-judgment can extend to the social. Those who breach certain codes of honor are disrespected, even condemned. Pride, on the other hand, is trickier. Though pride is 'shame's opposite' and may seem 'especially apt when you have done something out of the ordinary', Appiah remarks that 'an honorable person will often think that what he has done is simply what he had to do' (HC: 17). No sense of pride is involved. Overt and unchecked pride can, of course, lead to arrogance and hubris—undesirable and disrespectful qualities in a person. Overall, the honorable person is concerned with upholding the principle of honor itself in a self-motivated fashion, without consideration for the social or material gains that might be earned by being perceived as honorable.

Still, social circumstances are not irrelevant. Returning to the notion of culturally determined 'honor codes', Appiah points out that context is essential for understanding their criteria. He refers to this context as an 'honor world' (HC: 20). Members of an 'honor world' are 'honor peers' (HC: 88, 176). 'To say that people have honor is to say that they are entitled to respect according to the codes of their honor world', Appiah writes (HC: 20). This situation explains why those who committed murder through the practice of dueling were rarely prosecuted to the full extent of the law. It was understood that honor motivated the situation, not unreason. As Appiah quips, 'Dueling was one way of literally getting away with murder' (HC: 22). Nonetheless, opposition to this practice of 'judicial combat' did exist. Members of the clergy saw it as a violation of the Old Testament commandment not to kill. From the internal standpoint of dueling's 'honor world', questions gradually emerged about continuing the practice on grounds of pure rationality. Engaging in duels was seen as either 'brave or foolhardy', given the danger involved.

The shift away from dueling from a legal standpoint can be attributed to increasing intervention of the state and law in private conflicts. As Appiah describes, dueling was intended to discourage ill-mannered behavior. Ideally, it acted as a deterrent, but this prospect was never guaranteed. Furthermore, the death of one person to defend the honor of another person did not necessarily contribute to political order and a greater public good. Only public institutions could administer punishment in a way that could account for and ensure justice at a societal level. In short, the limited capacity of the law up through the early 19th century contributed to the persistence of dueling as a practice. In his *Lectures on Jurisprudence* (1763), Adam Smith argued that existing law did 'not protect men sufficiently from the affronts to honor that lead to challenges' (HC: 34). But the eventual legal changes of the 19th century do not completely explain the shifting fortunes of dueling's honor world.

Returning to Appiah's initial story, the duel between the Duke of Wellington and the Earl of Winchilsea ended with no one fatally shot, but neither was it a draw. After a brief negotiation, Winchilsea issued Wellington a written apology. But more significant was the fact that the press caught wind of the duel and subjected it to mockery in the emergent public sphere of popular media. Appiah remarks, 'The rise of a popular press and of working-class literacy made it increasingly clear—and, as democratic sentiment grew, increasingly unacceptable—that gentlemen were living outside the law' (HC: 38). The court of public opinion and its ideas about honor, therefore, played a vital role, in addition to the growing momentum for greater legal oversight over interpersonal affairs. The rise of a new business class that had profited from the spoils of imperialism and industrialization also had an impact. This new class sought to end the political control that the landowning aristocracy had wielded, whose members included the Duke of Wellington and the Earl of Winchilsea. The outcome of this growing social pluralism was the end of a preceding honor world and its cloistered codes that had little meaning in the new, wider world that was coming into being. Appiah notes that one of the last recorded duels, resulting in the death of one opponent, was recorded in 1852. Though dueling had persisted in the face of its illegality in the eyes of the Church, state, and public, it reached its end once the disrespect and shame involved became greater in meaning than the honor code and honor world that had sustained it.

NATIONAL HONOR

Appiah takes a different approach to honor and honor worlds when he examines the practice of footbinding in China and how it came to an end as a matter of national, rather than personal or class, honor. Honor codes once more are tied to identity. In this case, China's national identity was the identity of importance. Dueling illustrates how members of a group perceived themselves—an internal perspective among group members or 'honor peers'—but the story of footbinding reveals more fully how outsiders can perceive a group and influence its honor world. In this example, Chinese elites considered their national honor to be at stake in a new global landscape. As Appiah writes, 'Plainly, we may both gain and lose honor through the successes and failures of those with whom we share an identity' (HC: 64).

The long-held practice of footbinding had been a matter of gendered honor during the preceding centuries, dating from at least the 10th century and extending across social classes. Not only did the 'golden lotuses' (bound feet) of Chinese women exemplify female beauty, but the practice itself was also connected to sexual control—a woman with bound feet could not physically stray. Footbinding was a physically brutal process, causing immense pain and resulting in permanent bodily damage for girls and women. Similar to dueling, the moral arguments against it were clear well before the practice itself ended. The outcry that it aroused in Chinese society preceded political intervention.

Similar to the downfall of dueling in Britain, social and economic modernization played a role in the demise of footbinding. China's interactions with Europe had existed for centuries, but the modern period marked a turning point of internal societal change with the rise of European imperialism and global capitalism abetted by the speed and mobility of modern technology. The Opium Wars of the mid-19th century (1839–42 and 1856–60) were pivotal moments in this relationship, leading China to seek an end to the opium trade conducted by the British, who imported it from colonial India. The outcome of these two conflicts resulted in China's defeat and greater Western influence over its affairs, extending to its cultural norms and beliefs. Though they had had a presence in China since the 16th century, Christian missionaries proved instrumental. As Appiah describes, it was their 'modernizing Christianity, with its vision of science and technology in the service of human needs, that the modernizing literati [of China] responded to' (HC: 84). Indeed, as he notes, the secular cultural influence of missionaries proved greater than their ability to produce converts to the Christian faith.

The new intellectual elite in China that came of age during the 19th century was not only receptive to Western technology, media, and ideas, but they were also able to compare China's status to those of other countries in the world. 'The honor world of Chinese intellectuals at the start of the nineteenth century didn't include people elsewhere', Appiah observes, but by the end of the century that was no longer the case. 'Now their honor world included the Japanese, Europeans, and Americans whose critical evaluations undermined China's claim to respect' (HC: 88). The tensions over this change in outlook between older, conservative intellectuals and younger, more progressive intellectuals culminated in another political crisis similar to the Opium Wars—in this instance, the Boxer Rebellion (1899–1901), which also retained xenophobic and anti-imperial elements. It was also far more complicated given its populist roots and the multinational loyalties of those involved. For Appiah's purpose, the aftermath resulted in further reform and by 1912 the end of the imperial Qing Dynasty (1644–1912). Sun Yat-sen (1866–1925), the first president of the Republic of China, issued 'an order banning footbinding as a cruel and destructive custom' (HC: 91).

This backdrop of political change and transformation does not by itself explain why footbinding declined and eventually ended. The connection between private practices and public perception can be murky. Indeed, individuals may not always feel obligated to uphold the ideals and image of the political community to which they belong. Conversely, a state may not see itself as responsible for the behavior of its citizens. Appiah dwells on these opposing perspectives, asking, 'why should *my* worth be tied up with the worth of things done in the name of my nation?' (his emphasis, HC: 93) An answer to this question is that people, whether they like it or not, are identified with certain social groups and political communities, and these collective identities can impact the honor or shame of individual members, whether those individuals participate directly in a practice or not. Appiah notes that this individual conscription into a group is not necessarily a bad thing. The importance of group honor can motivate individual action, especially when reputation and respect in the eyes of others are involved. An Olympic athlete, for example, may feel a greater commitment to success when a nation's respect is at stake, not just their personal honor.

In the case of footbinding, Chinese intellectuals of the late 19th and early 20th centuries believed that this premodern practice brought disgrace to their country at a time when it sought to demonstrate its autonomy and modernity in a plural world. Politicians eventually agreed, even though the enforcement of the law and the practice's complete decline would take decades (Ko

2005). Ethics therefore preceded politics. More specifically, in this case, as with dueling, ethics encouraged and enabled political change to take hold. The abolition of footbinding illustrates once more how honor worlds and the honor codes that define them are not immune from outside influence, despite their long history. The view of footbinding as immoral, given its debilitating physical violence toward women, ultimately informed the political and legal action that outlawed the practice. The question and application of individual ethics became the wellspring of a broader moral revolution.

DIGNITY

These first two examples illuminate the dynamics of honor worlds among male elites and among nations. Appiah's next two examples examine the capacity for honor to inspire moral revolutions within transnational communities. His first example is the abolition of slavery in the Atlantic world. He specifically focuses on British abolitionism, since American, French, Spanish, Portuguese, and Dutch involvement in the trade and practice occupied different timelines. In the case of the British Empire, the slave trade ended in 1807 with the practice of slavery ending by 1834. There have been a number of explanations for this seismic shift—a profound one given that slavery in the Atlantic world had lasted since the 15th century. As summarized by Appiah, the motivations for this radical transition have ranged from economic explanations that slave production was no longer profitable (Williams 1944) to the momentum of moral arguments that garnered wide public support to end the trade and practice (Brown 2006). The former have addressed the profitability and fiscal costs of an economic systemic dependent on human bondage and forced labor. The latter have addressed the moral costs of the systemic dehumanization of African men, women, and children for over three centuries.

Similar to the preceding examples of dueling and footbinding, the perspective that the slave trade was immoral preceded its abolition. The question is how this moral view became widely accepted enough to enact new laws. One explanation is the role of Christianity and Christian 'virtue' specifically. William Wilberforce (1759–1833), a key leader of the British abolitionist movement, was an evangelical Christian for whom, in Appiah's words, 'there was no place for honor independent of religion and morality' (HC: 116). This fixing of honor to religious virtue at the level of the individual could extend to the nation, leading to 'Wilberforce's regular insistence that Britain's support for slavery undermined its claim to be a Christian nation' (HC: 118). This concern for national honor is analogous to that found in China over footbinding. Equally important for Appiah, however, was the rise of an industrial working class in Britain whose identity was linked to the dignity of labor.

Drawing upon E. P. Thompson's classic history *The Making of the English Working Class* (1963), Appiah argues that the emergence of workingmen's associations produced a new notion of 'dignity' centered on labor. This dignity was based on 'recognition respect' described earlier, rather than the more competitive 'appraisal respect' based on personal accomplishment. The foregrounding of recognition respect and dignity for working people, which had received little attention before, was 'a radical proposition' (HC: 131). Though national honor and Christian virtue played significant roles in defining the moral underpinnings of the abolitionist movement, Appiah emphasizes 'the dignity of labor among the laboring classes', though less recognized, was also a vital factor in securing popular, transnational support for the abolition of slavery (HC: 134). Racial differences between white British workers and Black slaves and freemen did not divide interests in his assessment. In contrast to the elites in his first two examples, Appiah makes the case that honor codes and honor worlds among the working classes, whether free or enslaved, could also contribute to moral revolutions.

Dignity is not only a theme across classes. It is also a theme across genders. The fourth revolution that Appiah examines is an ongoing one—the problem of 'honor killings' in certain parts of the world. He focuses in particular on Pakistan. Similar to footbinding, it is a highly gendered practice, and the moral stakes are even clearer given the unambiguous element of homicide. As with the preceding three case studies, the immorality of honor killing is well established, whether framed in the normative rules of national law in Pakistan and elsewhere or through *sharia*, the rules and dictates of Islamic law. Akin to slavery, its immorality can be understood on secular and religious grounds. Nonetheless, it has persisted among both urbanites and rural peasants alike. Similar to dueling, it is recognized as illegal, but often conducted with impunity. That honor killings endure in the face of arguments against them can once more be explained in terms of the 'honor codes' that give identity and a set of protocols for certain communities. One of Appiah's examples concerns an affluent Pakistani woman who was murdered by a hitman, paid for by her parents, because she sought a divorce from her husband. While her reasons for divorce were straightforward given the length of their separation, her parents felt her actions dishonored them and their identity as a family with social standing, leading to their fateful decision.

Appiah's consequent focus is on how this practice might end. Given that 'honor killings' are based on a preexisting 'honor code' and that the immorality is explicit, he stresses the relationship between identity and honor in particular as a vulnerability that can be exploited to demand the practice's termination. There are two reasons for this approach. 'First, a code of honor shapes your options by fixing what they require a person of your identity to do. It determines a set of honor practices', Appiah writes. 'And second, a code allows you to share in honor deriving from the achievements of others whose identity you share' (HC: 162). Put simply, the tandem of honor and identity works on two levels. Identity provides a set of instructions for garnering respect and honor as an individual. Identity also provides membership in a group, which allows one to share in the respect and honor of an identity group. This scenario is similar to dueling among the British aristocracy. Identity and honor can therefore cut both ways: the disrespectful or dishonorable behavior of an individual or group of individuals can make the whole group look bad. Honor codes and their honor worlds can subsequently end through the persistence of campaigns that highlight their immorality.

It follows that 'collective shaming' can be mobilized to end honor killings—an option at once feasible given the practice's immorality, but also difficult given its widespread practice across South Asia and the Middle East. As Appiah notes,

'Collective shaming requires a coalition of insiders and outsiders if it is to work' (HC: 166). This coalition can be constructed in part through what he calls 'symbolic affiliation', which encourages 'outsiders' to see that they have a stake in the matter because the practice among 'insiders' affects their own sense of honor (HC: 166). This type of solidarity is akin to the British working class who supported the abolition of slavery. In the case of honor killings, women in different countries can foster this kind of solidarity, whose criticism and outrage against honor killings can form part of a broader transnational effort against gender violence. Concurrent to collective shaming is the tactic of changing 'the grounds of honor, to alter the codes by which it is allocated' (HC: 169). Here, the case of dueling is useful, since it demonstrates how the basis for maintaining personal honor—killing another person—was gradually made the subject of public disrespect and private dishonor, in addition to being illegal and immoral. Though senses of honor can be surprisingly slow to change in comparison to law and morality, it is important nonetheless that such social transformations are pursued.

As Appiah summarizes, the concept of honor can introduce new ways of thinking about identity and its relationship to individual ethics and morality in the public sphere. In the case of honor killings, this situation, which ties respect and honor to patriarchal norms, can be reformed by introducing honor codes that emphasize alternative aspects of masculine identity. More importantly, the empowerment of women can displace an existing honor world that is shaped by masculinity. New honor codes for women, men, and families alike are possible. 'An *honor code* says how people of certain identities can gain the right to respect, how they can lose it, and how having and losing honor changes the way they should be treated', Appiah writes (his emphasis, HC: 175). Honor, in short, can determine behavior. It can 'bind the private and the public together' (HC: 178). By extension, it can encourage and sustain our responsibilities toward others and, in doing so, make our ethical selves better in the process.

Still, a distinction should be maintained between honor and morality. After all, honor codes typically lag behind new understandings of morality. Why is this the case? One answer is that the public recognition that honor bestows can be more tempting and a truer determinant of behavior than private ethical virtue. Appiah cites Kant's argument in *Groundwork of the Metaphysics of Morals* (1785)—that 'good will' consists of doing the right thing because it is the right thing—to mark a distinction between making choices for reasons of moral purpose (ethics) versus making choices for reasons of public recognition (honor). For Kant, the former approach of making choices for reasons of moral purpose exemplifies 'good will', which he favors. The latter approach is undertaken for the sole purpose of attaining respect and honor, which may not be grounded in ethical behavior, but is still more appealing to many people. Dueling and honor killings, once more, are examples of this disjuncture between honor and ethics. When honor and ethics do coincide, Kant uses the word *glücklicherweise* ('fortunately'), a term that suggests infrequency and unnatural concurrence. Under these rare circumstances, honor and ethics need not be identical, but they should be compatible. It remains possible that honor codes, being that they depend on public recognition to earn respect, can encourage the kind of ethical behavior that leads to a greater moral good. Yet this situation is not as common as one would hope.

Honor, it seems, is rarely honorable. Honor codes often depend upon and reinforce hierarchies—class, gender, and racial among them. What is equally distressing, as indicated by the case studies Appiah explores, is that honor codes are often defined and sustained by violence, whether the honor of men among English aristocrats or the honor of patriarchal families in South Asia and the Middle East. Nonetheless, Appiah believes that honor codes, suitably revised to reflect upstanding moral standards, can do more than individual ethical behavior alone. As he puts it,

> honor is no decaying vestige of a premodern order; it is, for us, what it has always been, an engine, fueled by the dialogue between our self-conceptions and the regard of others, that can drive us to take seriously our responsibilities in a world we share.
>
> (HC: 179)

Or, as he states more succinctly, 'Honor takes integrity public' (HC: 179). What is less clear is whether moral revolutions are sustainable and whether they are enough.

COUNTERARGUMENTS TO APPIAH

Appiah's argument for the role of honor codes, honor worlds, and moral revolutions points to a realm of ethical decisions and moral imagination deserving of greater attention. Revolutions tend to be understood as statist in orientation, whether the overthrow of Louis the XVI (1754–93) and the *Ancien Régime* during the French Revolution or decolonization in Africa and Asia during the 20th century. *The Honor Code* supplements these examples of political change by accenting the moral imagination and how transformation can occur without the physical struggle and violence of these mainstream cases of revolution. Yet, this alternative approach and paradigm leave a number of questions unanswered, several of which are addressed here.

One initial question is whether 'revolution' is the correct term. As cited earlier, Appiah defines 'revolution' as 'a large change in a short time', but this definition raises questions of scale and meaning. Did the end of dueling, for example, constitute a 'revolution'? Certainly, the practice died out indicating a change in attitudes about honor. But these views were held by a small section of British society. Should demographic size play a role in defining 'revolution'? Appiah's discussion of the English working class advances this question from another angle. While ending the slave trade was revolutionary, was the involvement of English workers vital to this endeavor? Their opinion appears essential in the British Isles, though their importance becomes smaller when a greater context is considered. Historians would argue that slave resistance and Black abolitionists, for example, played a more significant role. The examples of dueling and slavery also raise the question of incompletion. Though dueling has ended among British elites, the practice of 'judicial combat' persists in different parts of the world, especially where justice administered by the state is either absent or thought to be biased. Informal settlements in South Africa, favelas in Brazil, and low-income neighborhoods in the US still experience this kind of violence. Mafia violence among elites in Italy is another, albeit oft-romanticized, extra-judicial example, which Appiah does briefly touch upon. Even the case of slavery points to the problem of unfinished moral revolutions. Although the transatlantic trade has ended, slavery still continues in parts of the world through new forms of bondage and exploitation. Anti-Black racism and white violence continue. Moral revolutions, in sum, can be highly local and temporary. The definition and claims of 'moral revolution' need to be outlined carefully.

Another set of questions arises regarding the logic and chronology of moral revolutions. Revisiting the cases of dueling and honor killings, why do honor codes lag behind the law? And what is it about the law that limits its effectiveness in changing notions of honor? Why isn't the law and its presumed honor world enough to influence and change honor worlds that go against its dictates? This disjuncture between knowing a behavior is wrong and actually changing it suggests a cognitive dissonance that is still hard to explain. Appiah's response would likely be that culture, tradition, and their association with identity—amounting to circumstances of 'situation' ethics—can constrain the possibility of rapid change in honor worlds. But this explanation leaves open the question as to why moral and legal changes typically precede the revision or ending of honor codes. What honor world fostered moral and legal change in the first place? Why isn't this honor world powerful enough to transform those that are malignant? The role of 'virtue' ethics and the competition and hierarchies of power between coexisting honor worlds need further examination. While it is clear that honor can foster positive change, as in the case of footbinding in China, it is also clear that existing honor codes can impede progress, as in the case of honor killings. Yet even with the example of footbinding, the immorality of gender violence and patriarchal norms continued in China, if in different forms. In the end, nobody embraces an identity for its dishonorable qualities. We only embrace identity in the hope that we might partake in whatever honor it offers us, an idealistic aspiration that neglects the moral inconsistency of identities and how they can lead us into ethical problems.

Two literary examples point to further complexities. Achebe's novel *Things Fall Apart* as cited earlier can be framed by the idea of honor codes and honor worlds. Okonkwo, the main protagonist, is a beneficiary of an honor world that places a premium on his skills and identification with wrestling—a warrior paradigm that exists in many societies. However, this honor world and its

stability are gradually eroded, beginning with Okonkwo's killing of his adopted son, Ikemefuna, per the dictate of a local
oracle. Okonkwo's life unravels further when he and his family are forced into exile after the accidental death of another
villager. Soon after, his son, Nwoye, converts to Christianity.
The arrival of Christian missionaries and, eventually, British
colonial rule are the final undoing of Okonkwo's world and the
multiple senses of honor and respect attached to it. After failing
to organize a revolt against the British and killing a court offi-
cial in the process, Okonkwo tragically commits suicide at the
end of the novel—a direct result of these circumstances and his
inability to adapt. In contrast to Appiah's examples, *Things Fall
Apart* underscores how the end of honor worlds can culminate
in tragedy. Moral revolutions are a matter of perspective. They
may witness the beneficial end of honor codes and their worlds,
but they may also mark the end of identities and values of profound meaning.

Another example is the novel *Disgrace* (1999) by the South
African writer and Nobel Laureate J. M. Coetzee. The title itself
indicates how this work can be framed by Appiah's approach.
Disgrace concerns the fate of David Lurie, a white, middle-aged
South African man during the early post-apartheid period. Lurie
loses his job as a university professor after he has a non-con-
sensual relationship with an undergraduate student. Retreating
to the farm of his daughter, he falls victim to an attack that
results in serious injuries for him and in her being raped. His
story is similar to that of Okonkwo in the sense that the honor
world to which he belonged—defined by white male privilege
under the apartheid regime—has collapsed in the wake of the
end of apartheid. Unlike Okonkwo's situation, the demise of
this honor world is a positive change, a moral revolution in the
best sense. However, Coetzee's depiction of Lurie also reveals
how such shifts can leave individuals unprepared or unwilling
to negotiate the new terms for redefining their ethical selves and
their moral worlds. Though Lurie comes to terms with his post-
apartheid life, questions of justice at the personal and societal
level remain unresolved. Another kind of tragedy is therefore at
work—not the tragedy of the end of an honor world, as in the

case of Okonkwo, but the realization that renewed personal dignity through reconciliation with one's family and peers—and a reconciliation with one's own past actions—may not be possible. Moral revolutions can leave people behind, even those most in need of ethical repair.

IDEALS AND IDEALIZATION

If the idea of 'moral revolution' faces the prospect of revision when new evidence is marshaled, Appiah would likely respond by saying that is natural, that philosophers think in ideal terms. Concepts cannot account for every detail or for every historical circumstance. His short book *As If: Idealization and Ideals* (2017) complements his work on honor codes and moral revolutions by pointing out how many theories of politics, culture, race, and existence are in fact idealizations. As with honor worlds and their malignant dimensions, there is a disjuncture between how things are said to be and how things actually are. This disconnect is common in everyday life—one may go to church or synagogue, but not strictly abide by the Ten Commandments. Such ordinary experiences do not require the explanatory rigor of academic argument on every occasion. Still, this type of situation is a source of concern for a philosopher. How can we abide by such half-truths or, in some cases, complete fabrications?

Appiah draws from several thinkers to work through the question of idealization, including the Scottish Enlightenment philosopher David Hume (1711–76), who addressed what he referred to as the 'is-ought' problem (also known as Hume's Law). This problem marks a distinction between the world as it 'is' and the world as it 'ought to be'. More specifically, it highlights the difficulty of moving from factual observations about the world, as it is, toward prescriptive moral statements about how the world should ideally be. Hume was highly skeptical of speculative notions that lacked a grounded logical progression from factual statements: a leap of faith is ultimately required since any future outcome cannot be factually observed. Of greater influence on Appiah's thinking is the German philosopher Hans Vaihinger (1852–1933), whose work *The Philosophy of 'As If'* (1911) repositions Hume's line of thought to ask if unverifiable or patently false assertions can nonetheless be 'useful fictions'. As Appiah writes, Vaihinger is concerned with 'the role of untruth in *thinking* about reality' (his emphasis, AI: 4). To put it in terms that Hume would understand, it may not be possible to factually observe, let alone confirm, the future. But that may not be necessary. A leap of faith can be enough for ethical decision-making.

What is significant here, and a contrast from Appiah's earlier positions against the inconsistency and falsehood of identities, is how he accepts and argues for certain social fictions. In Appiah's words, 'an idealization is a useful untruth' (AI: 5). He quotes Vaihinger in an elaboration of this idea,

> It must be remembered that the object of the world of ideas as a whole is not the portrayal of reality—this would be an utterly impossible task— but rather to provide an *instrument for finding our way about more easily in the world.*

> (his emphasis, AI: 5)

As Appiah puts it succinctly, a theory is meant to be 'an instrument for managing reality, not a mirror held up to the world' (AI: 27). It is in the political realm that ideals and idealization can be seen perhaps most clearly. Appiah discusses how John Rawls's *A Theory of Justice* employs 'ideal theory' as a means of grasping systemic issues (AI: 116). Theoretical shorthand can be useful to map possible positions and solutions. However, its detachment from ground-level complexities, such as the specifics of race and gender inequality, can also leave it vulnerable to criticism (Anderson 2013; Mills 2005). Working with an idealization can therefore structure both debate and revision.

If the fiction of political idealization enables us to see the world beyond its complexities, it can equally direct personal decision-making. To paraphrase an example offered by Appiah, we agree that lying is ethically wrong, and yet we do it from time to time. Still, it is important to maintain the ideal that we should always tell the truth since it provides an ethical compass for decision-making, even if we break the rules occasionally.

Such ideals provide shortcuts for decisions in a variety of situations and settings. We do not have to parse situations or reinvent ethical choices on each and every occasion. This fiction—that we always tell the truth—provides general guidance and a principle to which we can aspire. The important takeaway is that the world is full of idealizations, and many of these fictions are useful in the sense that they can motivate moral behavior. As Appiah puts it, 'In believing that it is *as if* something is so, I dispose myself to act in a certain way' (his emphasis, AI: 22).

But fictions can of course cause problems, particularly when it comes to identity. Race, for example, is false on a scientific basis, and yet it remains a useful fiction for community formation, history, and politics. Still, measures like racial segregation, employment discrimination, and so forth have exploited this fiction. Ideal types can give us models to emulate, but they can also harden into stereotypes and instigate pejorative treatment. Furthermore, some ideals—ending world hunger—may be too distant or ideal, if you will, to be achieved in the short term. Such aspirations require an incremental approach to make them more achievable. Yet, despite the pragmatism at work, Appiah expresses skepticism—should moral ideals be compromised for the sake of expediency? Flexible policies and attainable goals are important, though moral ideals should not be mitigated to meet these ends. The fiction should perhaps remain. As a counterargument, Appiah draws from Amartya Sen to suggest that we should simply 'compare our current situation in imagination with a different situation and judge one of them better' (AI: 167). Sen's point is that you need not have a universal ideal as a starting point, or at all, to make moral decisions. Attention to local material conditions, such as poverty, can be enough to motivate a desire for change (Sen 1999, 2009).

CONCLUSIONS

This chapter has examined two approaches that Appiah has explored which can contribute to ethical behavior, a broader moral imagination, and benefit society at large. The first regards honor codes and the honor worlds they represent. These honor codes can promote ethical behavior through ideas of honor and public respect—as well as analogous fears of shame and disrepute—that can act as social guardrails limiting selfish or unethical behavior. Yet, as pointed out, this approach possesses limits. Notions of honor and shame can result not only in physical violence, as in the case of honor killings, but also psychologically damaging and traumatic abuse, as in the case of online 'call-out' culture today or the social normalization of 'body shaming'. In short, honor practices can reinforce existing hierarchies and political status quos with moral revolutions occurring only when their codes are seen as out of date or when positive codes of honor, like dignity for workers, are established and reinforced. Moral revolutions, though often less visible, can provide a complement to political revolutions, demonstrating the possibilities of transformation through ethical self-reflection and moral imagination.

Another path to change is through ideals and idealization. Appiah addresses how ideals such as freedom or equality, despite their fictional nature in everyday life, are useful for setting ethical standards and moral aims at a societal level. In answer to the question of why we would believe something we know to be false, Appiah repeats the conclusions of Vaihinger to say, 'an idealization involves ignoring the truth in a way that is useful for some purpose' (AI: 170). Or, as he puts it with even greater force, 'in taking something false for true, we are engaging what is, at least from one angle, our most astonishing human capacity: the ability to access ways the world is not but might have been' (AI: 171). This approach of believing in and moving toward 'truth in possible worlds' may incur criticism from those who believe that systemic change requires more than just ideals and a political imagination of idealization (AI: 172). Appiah's response to such critics would likely be that before such social change can be achieved, ethical decisions at the individual level are essential first. They serve as the starting point for politics.

AFTER APPIAH

Appiah writes in the preface to *The Honor Code*,

> I have spent a good deal of my scholarly life trying to get my fellow philosophers to recognize both the theoretical and the practical importance of things that they may have taken too little notice of: race and ethnicity, gender and sexuality, nationality and religion ... all of the rich social identities with which we make our lives.
>
> (HC: xv)

In *The Ethics of Identity*, he puts his professional concerns even more succinctly by stating that 'identity is at the heart of human life' (EI: 268). Appiah has positioned the issue of 'identity' and the ethical and moral questions surrounding it as the central theme of his work. There is a recurring tension in his books between respecting identity and deconstructing it. He has remained committed to creating a space for critical reasoning to point out the inconsistencies of identity. As a consequence, a distinction can be drawn in his work between ethical and political worlds. Appiah places ethics ahead of politics. He is more interested in diagnostics—the analysis of social truths and untruths—than he is with proposing solutions in the realm of policy.

But politics are not entirely absent from his work. Appiah has embraced an Anglophone liberal tradition due to its concerns with identity and individual freedom. Indeed, Appiah is an interesting case study within current debates over the crisis of liberalism (Deneen 2018; Fawcett 2018), which have underscored the limits of liberalism in addressing structural inequalities along race, class, and gendered lines. Black philosophers like Charles W. Mills have been particularly vocal about the shortcomings of liberal approaches to achieving racial justice (Mills 2017). Appiah's approval of John Stuart Mill and British liberalism might be seen as promoting a Eurocentric political tradition, despite his critiques of Eurocentrism on other occasions. Appiah has largely taken an anti-historicist view of the liberal tradition by not fully reckoning with its imperial origins.

This intellectual decision can be traced, in part, to his personal history as discussed in this book. Many of Appiah's positions can be understood as an effect of decolonization and its complex aftermath. Indeed, the liberal tradition itself materialized out of a historical composite of decolonization in the Americas, conditions in post-revolutionary Europe, and the rise of new forms of imperialism in the nineteenth century. Specific to postcolonial Ghana, Appiah has written,

> My father saw the colonial state's abuses of his fellows (and himself) and, in particular, the refusal to pay them the respect that was their due. As a lawyer and a member of the opposition, he traveled Ghana in the years after independence defending people whose rights were being abused by the postcolonial state. The political tradition of liberalism flows from these experiences of illiberal government.
>
> (EI: 270)

Appiah's espousal of this political tradition, therefore, has as much to do with personal experience as it does with formal academic study. As he further summarizes, 'the persecution of political dissenters by postcolonial despots has made protection of political dissent central to the liberalism of those who resist postcolonial states in Africa' (EI: 270). Appiah's politics thus conform to what can be called a 'postcolonial liberalism' (see also Ivison 2002). Acknowledgment and judicious examination of other liberal traditions around the world are needed in order to diversify what we mean by 'liberalism'.

What makes Appiah's positions particularly striking is that they mark a generational contrast from the ideas of anti-colonial nationalism, Pan-Africanism, and Marxism-Leninism promoted by Kwame Nkrumah and his continental cohort of revolutionary activist-intellectuals. Appiah's critiques of race and Pan-African thought in *In My Father's House* may appear to be solely academic, but it is more useful to situate them historically as a philosopher's attempt to point to the limitations of these ideas after decolonization and at the end of the twentieth century. This interpretation is not to argue that readers should agree with Appiah, but it is important to understand his motivations. Not only did the group politics of his father's generation have less practical immediacy for Appiah, given his upbringing after a revolutionary period, but, as a result of this fact, Appiah has had to face a different set of questions about individual rights and ethics after revolution or, in this instance, decolonization. His embrace of liberalism did not appear out of thin air. The failures of African socialism combined with the political distortions of race, nationalism, and nativism in post-colonial Africa have led to patterns of political exclusion, silence, and violence. Things fell apart again in new ways and under different circumstances. For ethical and moral reasons, Appiah has remained a skeptic of these identities and the ideologies that have buttressed them. In his own words, 'Ideologies succeed to the extent that they are invisible, in the moment that their fretwork of assumptions passes beneath consciousness; genuine victories are won without a shot being fired' (IMFH: 60). He has consequently taken up the task of exposing such ideologies as flawed.

There are grounds for arguing with Appiah. Critics have pointed to how his discussions of 'Africa' can tend toward essentialism, with little differentiation between former settler and non-settler colonies (Gibson 1995). Indeed, it is difficult to write about Appiah without slipping into such shorthand generalizations, as admittedly seen in this book. His regional attention is primarily confined to West Africa and Ghana specifically. Appiah has faced censure on his handling of culture and race in

Africa as a result (Gyekye 1995; Nzegwu 1996; Oyěwùmí 1997; Pierre 2012). His own acceptance of multiple identities has also been critiqued for demonstrating a lack of political commitment. As Katya Gibel Azoulay has written, 'constructive strategic essentialism does not negate the plurality of [a person's] identities and their mutability' (Azoulay 1996: 137). Going further, on some occasions, as with his discussion of African philosophy, he stresses the shallowness of colonialism. On other occasions, like his engagements with Soyinka, nativism, and the 'invention' of tradition, he emphasizes the ineluctable influence of colonialism. Indeed, his analysis of Soyinka (Chapter 3) and how he manages a fine line between explaining 'Africa' to non-African audiences and caretaking cultural detail for local African audiences can be applied to Appiah's own work. The Nigerian philosopher Sophie Oluwole (1935–2018) has reproached Appiah for not taking African thought, as articulated in African languages, more seriously (Oluwole 1997; see also Oyegoke 1996). Beyond these circumstances related to African studies, his invocations of religion and religious difference, which he refers to across several books, have been drawn too starkly for some readers, imparting a consensus of belief and a uniformity of practice and geography that may not reflect local circumstances. Lila Abu-Lughod has faulted his handling of Islam in *The Honor Code*, arguing that Appiah has contributed to a discourse of 'IslamLand' that emerged during the so-called 'War on Terror' (Abu-Lughod 2013; see also Friedman 2018).

Turning to his most significant contributions, Appiah, as noted in Chapter 2, has tended to employ a thin, semantic concept of race rather than the thick, sociohistorical version pioneered by Du Bois and other scholar-activists—a stance for which Appiah has faced criticism (Gordon 1995; Gordon 1997). Philosopher Paget Henry has written, 'For Appiah, the literal truth [that race is pseudoscience] is too often the logical truth' (Henry 1993: 78), leaving incompletely addressed the social and historical conditions that can provide reasons for embracing racial identity. Race should be understood as 'plural' in definition rather than 'unitary' (Lee 1994). Though it is understandable why he would be reticent about racial identity entirely, given his family background, Appiah has since revised his views to be anti-racist, rather than anti-'race', in recognition of the continued salience of 'race' as a social and political category (Appiah 1996b, 2008b, 2014, 2018). His argument for moral revolutions has also faced detractors due to the ambiguities of 'honor' and the limits of 'moral revolution' as noted earlier. Anti-Black racism and violence still continue over two centuries after the abolition of the British slave trade, underscoring the evolution of dehumanizing attitudes and practices rather than their end. Regarding his work on cosmopolitanism, Appiah's skepticism toward repatriating artwork appears out of step with current debates over restitution and efforts to 'decolonize' museum collections (Sarr and Savoy 2018). His leadership of the Modern Language Association in the US in 2016 and early 2017, when its membership voted against a boycott of Israel despite its prolonged occupation of East Jerusalem and the West Bank since the 1967 Six-Day War, its recent implementation of apartheid-style separation measures, and its mistreatment of Palestinians more generally, also produced withering condemnation from some quarters. In a statement conforming to his cosmopolitan ideals, Appiah explained that he was 'strongly opposed to all cultural boycotts' (Schuessler 2017). Yet the cosmopolitan ethic remains a source of debate (Archibugi 2003; Robbins et al. 2017).

Appiah is attentive to the limits of what academic knowledge can do when set against the backdrop of society at large. He makes this point in 'African Identities' from *In My Father's House*, in which he writes self-critically,

> But the facts I have been rehearsing should imbue us all with a strong sense of the marginality of such [academic] work to the central issue of the resistance to racism and ethnic violence—and to sexism, and to the other structures of difference that shape the world of power.

Instead, 'they [these facts] should force upon us the clear realization that the real battle is not being fought in the academy' (IMFH: 179). However, he expresses continued commitment to intellectual work as a core aspect of this struggle. Appiah further remarks,

> the shape of modern Africa (the shape of our world) is in large part the product, often the unintended and unanticipated product, of theories … We cannot change the world simply by evidence and reasoning, but we surely cannot change it without them either.

(IMFH: 179)

He reiterates these stances later in *Cosmopolitanism*, writing

> I am a philosopher. I believe in reason. But I have learned in a life of university teaching and research that even the cleverest people are not easily shifted by reason alone—and that can be true even in the most cerebral of realms.

(COS: 84)

This acknowledgment of limits contributes to the moral and political idealism that exists throughout his work. Taken as a whole, his intellectual project can be described as promoting a liberal humanism at the global level. One dimension of this effort is what he calls a 'tenable cosmopolitanism', which 'tempers a respect for difference with a respect for actual human beings' (COS: 113). This definition of cosmopolitanism accommodates his early observation that 'since it is too late for us [Africa and Europe] to escape each other, we might instead seek to turn to our advantage the mutual interdependencies history has thrust upon us' (IMFH: 72) and, furthermore, his belief that 'truth is the property of no culture … we should take the truths we need wherever we find them' (IMFH: 5). Appiah concedes that people live by certain fictions, and it is important to be aware of this— and, in contrast to his early work, to let such fictions stand, including race. As he writes in the conclusion to *As If*,

> let us just say that what matters is the truth about what is possible … we philosophers have a soft spot for truths, even if we have discovered that many of the most exciting and important things we think and say are not, strictly speaking, true at all.

(AI: 172)

Appiah ultimately makes a case for the importance of individual liberty, freedom of thought, and the significance of ethics and the moral imagination for approaching social and political questions. He is committed to these conditions of possibility and their roles in the construction of a meaningful life. As he summarizes in *The Ethics of Identity*,

> To create a life, in other words, is to interpret the materials that history has given you. Your character, your circumstances, your psychological constitution, including the beliefs and preferences generated by the interaction of your innate endowments and your experience: all these need to be taken into account in shaping a life. They are not constraints on that shaping; they are its materials.
>
> (EI: 163)

Appiah can be debated on the social, political, and material factors that define such agency in the creation of one's identity. But he is certainly not alone in his belief that freedom, ethics, and the importance of reason in negotiating questions of identity and political commitment matter. These are enduring ideas. Indeed, his personal identity, which marks a convergence of worlds, underscores the variety of possible materials for making one's life. Appiah's work invites conversation and debate on these issues that define our present and will shape our futures to come.

FURTHER READING

The following bibliography of books, edited collections, articles, and other publications provides a selection of Kwame Anthony Appiah's most significant works as of June 2020. It is not designed to be comprehensive, but it is intended to highlight contributions of particular interest for future reading. For more information, readers may want to consult Appiah's personal website (active as of 2020): http://appiah.net/

MAJOR WORKS (IN ORDER OF PUBLICATION)

Appiah, Kwame Anthony (1985) *Assertion and Conditionals*, Cambridge: Cambridge University Press.

—— (1986) *For Truth in Semantics*, Oxford: Blackwell.

—— (1992) *In My Father's House: Africa in the Philosophy of Culture*, New York: Oxford University Press.

—— (2005) *The Ethics of Identity*, Princeton: Princeton University Press.

—— (2006) *Cosmopolitanism: Ethics in a World of Strangers*, New York: W. W. Norton.

——— (2008) *Experiments in Ethics*, Cambridge, MA: Harvard University Press.

——— (2010) *The Honor Code: How Moral Revolutions Happen*, New York: W. W. Norton.

——— (2014) *Lines of Descent: W. E. B. Du Bois and the Emergence of Identity*, Cambridge, MA: Harvard University Press.

——— (2017) *As If: Idealization and Ideals*, Cambridge, MA: Harvard University Press.

——— (2018) *The Lies That Bind: Rethinking Identity*, New York: W. W. Norton.

CO-AUTHORED WORKS (IN ORDER OF PUBLICATION)

Appiah, Kwame Anthony and Amy Gutmann (1996) *Color Conscious: The Political Morality of Race*, Princeton: Princeton University Press.

Appiah, Kwame Anthony, Peggy Appiah, and Ivor Agyeman-Duah (2007) *Bu Me Bε: The Proverbs of the Akans*, Oxfordshire: Ayebia Clarke Publishing.

TEXTBOOKS (IN ORDER OF PUBLICATION)

Appiah, Kwame Anthony (1989) *Necessary Questions: An Introduction to Philosophy*, New York: Prentice-Hall.

——— (2003) *Thinking It Through: An Introduction to Contemporary Philosophy*, New York: Oxford University Press.

CO-EDITED WORKS (IN ORDER OF PUBLICATION)

Appiah, Kwame Anthony and Henry Louis Gates, Jr. (1992) *'Race', Writing, and Difference*, Chicago: University of Chicago Press.

—— (1993a) *Langston Hughes: Critical Perspectives Past and Present*, New York: Amistad Press.

—— (1993b) *Zora Neale Hurston: Critical Perspectives Past and Present*, New York: Amistad Press.

—— (1993c) *Toni Morrison: Critical Perspectives Past and Present*, New York: Amistad Press.

—— (1993d) *Alice Walker: Critical Perspectives Past and Present*, New York: Amistad Press.

—— (1993e) *Richard Wright: Critical Perspectives Past and Present*, New York: Amistad Press.

—— (1995) *Identities*, Chicago: University of Chicago Press.

—— (1996) *A Dictionary of Global Culture*, New York: Knopf.

—— (1999) *Encarta Africana*, Redmond, WA: Microsoft.

—— (2010) *The Encyclopedia of Africa*, New York: Oxford University Press.

Appiah, Kwame Anthony and Martin Bunzl (2007) *Buying Freedom: The Ethics and Economics of Slave Redemption*, Princeton: Princeton University Press.

NOVELS (IN ORDER OF PUBLICATION)

Appiah, Kwame Anthony (1990) *Avenging Angel*, London: Constable.

—— (1994) *Nobody Likes Letitia*, London: Constable.

—— (1995) *Another Death in Venice*, London: Constable.

MAJOR ARTICLES AND BOOK CHAPTERS (IN ORDER OF PUBLICATION)

Appiah, Kwame Anthony (1985) 'The Uncompleted Argument: Du Bois and the Illusion of Race', *Critical Inquiry* 12, no. 1: 21–37.

—————— (1986) 'Are We Ethnic? The Theory and Practice of American Pluralism', *Black American Literature Forum* 20, no. 1/2: 209–24.

—————— (1988) 'Out of Africa: Topologies of Nativism', *Yale Journal of Criticism* 2, no. 1: 153–78.

—————— (1989) 'The Conservation of "Race"', *Black American Literature Forum* 23, no. 1: 37–60.

—————— (1990a) 'Alexander Crummell and the Invention of Africa', *Massachusetts Review* 31, no. 3: 385–406.

—————— (1990b) 'Racisms', in *Anatomy of Racism*, edited by David Theo Goldberg, Minneapolis: University of Minnesota Press, 3–17.

—————— (1991a) 'Altered States', *Wilson Quarterly* 15, no. 1: 20–32.

—————— (1991b) 'Is the Post- in Postmodernism the Post- in Postcolonial?', *Critical Inquiry* 17, no. 2: 336–57.

—————— (1992a) 'Introduction', in *Things Fall Apart*, edited by Chinua Achebe, London: Everyman, ix–xvii.

—————— (1992b) 'Inventing an African Practice in Philosophy: Epistemological Issues', in *The Surreptitious Speech: Présence Africaine and the Politics of Otherness, 1947–1987*, edited by V.Y. Mudimbe, Chicago: University of Chicago Press, 227–37.

—————— (1993b) 'Thick Translation', *Callaloo* 16, no. 4: 808–19.

—————— (1994a) 'Loyalty to Humanity', *Boston Review*, November 1, http://bostonreview.net/philosophy-religion/anthony-appiah-loyalty-humanity

—————— (1994b) 'Myth, Literature and the African World', in *Wole Soyinka: An Appraisal*, edited by Adewale Maja-Pearce, London: Heinemann, 98–115.

—————— (1996a) 'Against National Culture', *English in Africa* 23, no. 1: 11–27.

———— (1996b) 'Reconstructing Racial Identities', *Research in African Literatures* 27, no. 3: 68–72.

———— (1997) 'Cosmopolitan Patriots', *Critical Inquiry* 23, no. 3: 617–39.

———— (1999) 'Preface', in *Racism*, edited by Albert Memmi, Minneapolis, MN: University of Minnesota Press, vii–x.

———— (2001a) 'Cosmopolitan Reading', in *Cosmopolitan Geographies: New Locations in Literature and Culture*, edited by Vinay Dharwadker, New York: Routledge, 197–227.

———— (2001b) 'Liberalism, Individuality, and Identity', *Critical Inquiry* 27, no. 2: 305–32.

———— (2003) 'Citizens of the World', in *Globalizing Rights: The Oxford Amnesty Lectures 1999*, edited by Matthew J. Gibney, Oxford: Oxford University Press, 189–232.

———— (2004) 'Comprendre les réparations: une réflexion préliminaire', *Cahiers d'Etudes africaines* XLIV, no. 1–2: 173–74, 25–40.

———— (2006a) 'Language Rights', *PMLA* 121, no. 5: 1618–20.

———— (2006b) 'The Politics of Identity', *Daedalus* 135, no. 4: 15–22.

———— (2008a) 'Bending Towards Justice', *Journal of Human Development* 9, no. 3: 343–55.

———— (2008b) 'Foreword', *Black Skin, White Masks*, edited by Frantz Fanon, translated by Richard Philcox, New York: Grove Press, vii–x.

———— (2009) 'Whose Culture Is It?', in *Whose Culture?: The Promise of Museums and the Debate over Antiquities*, edited by James Cuno, Princeton: Princeton University Press, 71–86.

———— (2010) 'Dignity and Global Duty', *Boston University Law Review* 90, no. 2: 661–75.

——— (2011) '"Group Rights" and Racial Affirmative Action', *The Journal of Ethics* 15, no. 3: 265–80.

——— (2013) 'The Democratic Spirit', *Daedalus* 142, no. 2: 209–21.

——— (2015) 'Race in the Modern World: The Problem of the Color Line', *Foreign Affairs* 94, no. 2: 1–8.

——— (2016) 'The Diversity of Diversity', in *Our Compelling Interests: The Value of Diversity for Democracy and a Prosperous Society*, edited by Earl Lewis and Nancy Cantor, Princeton: Princeton University Press, 161–69.

——— (2017) 'Foreword', *The African Trilogy: Things Fall Apart, Arrow of God, No Longer at Ease*, edited by Chinua Achebe, New York: Penguin, vii–xi.

Appiah, Kwame Anthony and V. Y. Mudimbe (1993a) 'The Impact of African Studies on Philosophy', in *Africa and the Disciplines: The Contributions of Research in Africa to the Social Sciences and Humanities*, edited by Robert H. Bates, V. Y. Mudimbe, and Jean F. O'Barr, Chicago: University of Chicago Press, 113–38.

CRITICISM

The following books and articles have engaged with Appiah's work in different ways. This selection is not comprehensive. Items are listed in alphabetical order by surname.

Azoulay, Katya Gibel (1996) 'Outside Our Parents' House: Race, Culture, and Identity', *Research in African Literatures* 27, no. 1: 129–42.

Gibson, Nigel (1995) 'Post-Colonial Ideological Battles', *Africa Today* 42, no. 3: 73–9.

Gordon, Lewis R. (1995) *Bad Faith and Antiblack Racism*, Amherst, NY: Humanity Books.

———— (1997) *Her Majesty's Other Children: Sketches of Racism from a Neocolonial Age*, Lanham, MD: Rowman & Littlefield.

———— (2008) *An Introduction to Africana Philosophy*, New York: Cambridge University Press.

Gyekye, Kwame (1995) *An Essay on African Philosophical Thought: The Akan Conceptual Scheme*, Philadelphia: Temple University Press.

Henry, Paget (1993) 'African Philosophy in the Mirror of Logicism: A Review/Essay', *The CLR James Journal* 4, no. 1: 70–8.

Klobah, Mahoumbah, Mawuena Logan, Dean Makuluni, Cherry Muhanji, and Theresa Riffe with Barbara Eckstein (1996) 'A Conversation about Kwame Anthony Appiah's In My Father's House: Africa in the Philosophy of Culture', *The Iowa Review* 26, no. 3: 1–26.

Nicol, Davidson (1993) 'Review Essay: Race, Ethnohistory and Other Matters: A Discussion of Kwame Anthony Appiah, *In My Father's House: Africa in the Philosophy of Culture*', *African Studies Review* 36, no. 3: 109–16.

Nzegwu, Nkiru (1996) 'Questions of Identity and Inheritance: A Critical Review of Kwame Anthony Appiah's *In My Father's House*', *Hypatia* 11, no. 1: 175–201.

Okafor, Victor O. (1993) 'An Afrocentric Critique of Appiah's *In My Father's House*', *Journal of Black Studies* 24, no. 2: 196–212.

Oluwole, Sophie (1997) 'The Cultural Enslavement of the African Mind', in *The Essentials of African Studies*, Vol. 1, edited by Sophie Oluwole, Lagos: General African Studies Programme, University of Lagos, 129–47.

Outlaw, Lucius (1996) '"Conserve" Races? In Defense of W. E. B. Du Bois', in *W. E. B. Du Bois on Race and Culture: Philosophy, Politics, and Poetics*, edited by Bernard W. Bell, Emily Grosholz, and James B. Stewart, New York: Routledge, 15–37.

Oyegoke, Lekan (1996) 'Leaky Mansion? Appiah's Theory of African Cultures', *Research in African Literatures* 27, no. 1: 143–48.

Oyěwùmí, Oyèrónké (1997) *The Invention of Women: Making an African Sense of Western Gender Discourses*, Minneapolis, MN: University of Minnesota Press.

Pierre, Jemima (2012) *The Predicament of Blackness: Postcolonial Ghana and the Politics of Race*, Chicago: University of Chicago Press.

Ramazani, Jahan (ed.) (2018) *On Kwame Anthony Appiah*, special issue of *New Literary History* 49, no. 2.

Serequeberhan, Tsenay (1996) 'Reflections on *In My Father's House*', *Research in African Literatures* 27, no. 1: 110–18.

Slaymaker, William (1996) 'Agents and Actors in African Antifoundational Aesthetics: Theory and Narrative in Appiah and Mudimbe', *Research in African Literatures* 27, no. 1: 119–28.

Tanoukhi, Nirvana (2008) 'The Scale of World Literature', *New Literary History* 39, no. 3: 599–617.

BIBLIOGRAPHY

Abu-Lughod, Lila (2013) *Do Muslim Women Need Saving?*, Cambridge, MA: Harvard University Press.

Achebe, Chinua (1977) 'An Image of Africa', *Massachusetts Review* 18, no. 4: 782–94.

—— (2010 [1958]) *Things Fall Apart*, New York: Penguin.

Adichie, Chimamanda Ngozi (2013) *Americanah: A Novel*, New York: Knopf.

Ahlman, Jeffrey S. (2017) *Living with Nkrumahism: Nation, State, and Pan-Africanism in Ghana*, Athens, OH: Ohio University Press.

Ahluwalia, Pal (2010) *Out of Africa: Post-Structuralism's Colonial Roots*, New York: Routledge.

Allman, Jean Marie (1990) 'The Youngmen and the Porcupine: Class, Nationalism and Asante's Struggle for Self-Determination, 1954–57', *The Journal of African History* 31, no. 2: 263–79.

———— (1993) *The Quills of the Porcupine: Asante Nationalism in an Emergent Ghana*, Madison, WI: University of Wisconsin Press.

Anderson, Benedict (1983) *Imagined Communities: Reflections on the Origin and Spread of Nationalism*, London: Verso.

Anderson, Elizabeth (2013) *The Imperative of Integration*, Princeton: Princeton University Press.

Appadurai, Arjun (1996) *Modernity at Large: Cultural Dimensions of Globalization*, Minneapolis, MN: University of Minnesota Press.

Appiah, Joseph (1990) *Joe Appiah: The Autobiography of an African Patriot*, foreword by Henry Louis Gates, Jr., London: Praeger.

Archibugi, Daniele (2003) *Debating Cosmopolitics*, London: Verso.

Azoulay, Katya Gibel (1996) 'Outside Our Parents' House: Race, Culture, and Identity', *Research in African Literatures* 27, no. 1: 129–42.

Balakrishnan, Sarah (2018) 'Afropolitanism and the End of Black Nationalism', in *Routledge International Handbook of Cosmopolitanism Studies*, edited by Gerard Delanty, London: Routledge, 575–85.

Baldwin, James (1992 [1963]) *The Fire Next Time*, New York: Vintage.

———— (2013 [1953]) *Go Tell It on the Mountain*, New York: Vintage.

de Beauvoir, Simone (2011 [1949]) *The Second Sex*, translated by Constance Borde and Sheila Malovany Chevallier, New York: Vintage.

Belich, James (2009) *Replenishing the Earth: The Settler Revolution and the Rise of the Angloworld, 1783–1939*, New York: Oxford University Press.

Bernabé, Jean, Patrick Chamoiseau, and Raphaël Confiant (1993) *Éloge de la Créolité / In Praise of Creoleness*, translated by Mohamed Bouya Taleb-Khyar, Paris: Gallimard.

Bernasconi, Robert (2009) '"Our Duty to Conserve": W. E. B. Du Bois's Philosophy of History in Context', *South Atlantic Quarterly* 108, no. 3: 519–40.

Bhabha, Homi K. (ed.) (1990) *Nation and Narration*, London: Routledge.

—— (1994) *The Location of Culture*, London: Routledge.

Biko, Steve (2002 [1978]) *I Write What I Like: Selected Writings*, edited by Aelred Stubbs, C. R., Chicago: University of Chicago Press.

Bloom, Allan (1987) *The Closing of the American Mind: How Higher Education Has Failed Democracy and Impoverished the Souls of Today's Students*, New York: Simon & Schuster.

Bloom, Harold (1994) *The Western Canon: The Books and School of the Ages*, New York: Harcourt Brace.

Boas, Franz (1982 [1940]) *Race, Language, and Culture*, Chicago: University of Chicago Press.

Bourdieu, Pierre (1977 [1972]) *Outline of a Theory of Practice*, translated by Richard Nice, Cambridge: Cambridge University Press.

Brantlinger, Patrick (1988) *Rule of Darkness: British Literature and Imperialism, 1830–1914*, Ithaca, NY: Cornell University Press.

Brennan, Timothy (1997) *At Home in the World: Cosmopolitanism Now*, Cambridge, MA: Harvard University Press.

Brizuela-Garcia, Esperanza (2014) 'Cosmopolitanism: Why Nineteenth Century Gold Coast Thinkers Matter in the Twenty-First Century', *Ghana Studies* 17: 203–21.

Brown, Christopher Leslie (2006) *Moral Capital: Foundations of British Abolitionism*, Chapel Hill: University of North Carolina Press.

Butler, Judith (2005) *Giving an Account of Oneself*, New York: Fordham University Press.

Caine, Barbara (2010) 'Writing Cosmopolitan Lives: Joseph and Kwame Anthony Appiah', *History Workshop Journal* 70: 152–71.

Chakrabarty, Dipesh (2000) *Provincializing Europe: Postcolonial Thought and Historical Difference*, Princeton: Princeton University Press.

Chatterjee, Partha (1986) *Nationalist Thought and the Colonial World: A Derivative Discourse?*, Minneapolis, MN: University of Minnesota Press.

Cleaver, Eldridge (1999 [1968]) *Soul on Ice*, New York: Delta.

Clifford, James (1988) *The Predicament of Culture: Twentieth-Century Ethnography, Literature, and Art*, Cambridge, MA: Harvard University Press.

Coetzee, Carli (ed.) (2017) *Afropolitanism: Reboot*, New York: Routledge.

Coetzee, J.M. (1999) *Disgrace: A Novel*, New York: Penguin.

Cohn, Bernard S. (1996) *Colonialism and Its Forms of Knowledge: The British in India*, Princeton: Princeton University Press.

Cole, Teju (2011) *Open City: A Novel*, New York: Random House.

Conrad, Joseph (2008 [1902]) *Heart of Darkness and Other Tales*, Oxford: Oxford University Press.

Cooper, Frederick (2005) *Colonialism in Question: Theory, Knowledge, History*, Berkeley: University of California Press.

Cornell, Drucilla, and Nyoko Muvangua (2012) 'Introduction: The Re-Cognition of *uBuntu*', in *uBuntu and the Law: African Ideals and Post-Apartheid Jurisprudence*, edited by

Drucilla Cornell and Nyoko Muvangua, New York: Fordham University Press, 1–27.

Dangarembga, Tsitsi (1988) *Nervous Conditions*, New York: Seal Press.

Davis, Angela Y. (1974) *Angela Davis: An Autobiography*, New York: Random House.

———— (1981) *Women, Race & Class*, New York: Random House.

Deneen, Patrick J. (2018) *Why Liberalism Failed*, New Haven: Yale University Press.

Diagne, Souleymane Bachir (2012) *African Art as Philosophy: Senghor, Bergson and the Idea of Negritude*, translated by Chike Jeffers, London: Seagull Books.

Du Bois, W. E. B. (1899) *The Philadelphia Negro: A Social Study*, Philadelphia: University of Pennsylvania Press.

———— (1915) *The Negro*, New York: Holt.

———— (1979 [1947]) *The World and Africa*, New York: International Publishers.

———— (1986) *Writings: The Suppression of the African Slave-Trade, The Souls of Black Folk, Dusk of Dawn, Essays and Articles*, edited by Nathan Huggins, New York: Library of America.

———— (1996a [1903]) 'The Talented Tenth', in *The Future of Race*, edited by Henry Louis Gates, Jr. and Cornel West, New York: Knopf, 133–58.

———— (1996b [1948]) 'The Talented Tenth Memorial Address', in *The Future of Race*, edited by Henry Louis Gates, Jr. and Cornel West, New York: Knopf, 159–77.

———— (1998 [1935]) *Black Reconstruction in America, 1860–1880*, New York: Free Press.

────── (2007 [1930]) *Africa, Its Geography, People and Products* and *Africa—Its Place in Modern History*, edited by Henry Louis Gates, Jr., New York: Oxford University Press.

────── (2011 [1903]) *The Negro Church*, Eugene, OR: Cascade Books.

Du Bois, W. E. B. and Joseph Fracchia (2006 [1906]) 'Die Negerfrage in den Vereinigten Staaten (The Negro Question in the United States) (1906)', *CR: The New Centennial Review* 6, no. 3: 241–90.

Dunbar-Ortiz, Roxanne (2014) *An Indigenous Peoples' History of the United States*, Boston: Beacon Press.

Dworkin, Ronald (2000) *Sovereign Virtue: Equality in Theory and Practice*, Cambridge, MA: Harvard University Press.

Eaglestone, Robert (1997) *Ethical Criticism: Reading After Levinas*, Edinburgh: Edinburgh University Press.

Ellison, Ralph (1995 [1952]) *Invisible Man*, New York: Vintage.

Fabian, Johannes (2002 [1983]) *Time and the Other: How Anthropology Makes Its Object*, New York: Columbia University Press.

Fanon, Frantz (2005 [1961]) *The Wretched of the Earth*, translated by Richard Philcox, New York: Grove.

────── (2008 [1952]) *Black Skin, White Masks*, translated by Richard Philcox, New York: Grove.

Fawcett, Edmund (2018 [2014]) *Liberalism: The Life of an Idea*, second edition, Princeton: Princeton University Press.

Feldman, Noah (2007) 'Cosmopolitan Law?', *The Yale Law Journal* 116, no. 5: 1022–70.

Fields, Karen E. and Barbara J. Fields (2012) *Racecraft: The Soul of Inequality in American Life*, London: Verso.

Foucault, Michel (1982 [1969]) *The Archaeology of Knowledge: And the Discourse on Language*, translated by A. M. Sheridan Smith, New York: Vintage.

—— (1990 [1978]) *The History of Sexuality, Volume 1: An Introduction*, translated by Robert Hurley, New York: Vintage.

—— (2008 [2004]) *The Birth of Biopolitics: Lectures at the Collège de France, 1978–1979*, edited by Michel Senellart, translated by Graham Burchell, New York: Picador.

Friedman, Susan Stanford (2018) 'Cosmopolitanism, Religion, Diaspora: Kwame Anthony Appiah and Contemporary Muslim Women's Writing', *New Literary History* 49, no. 2: 199–225.

Gates, Jr., Henry Louis (1987) *Figures in Black: Words, Signs, and the 'Racial' Self*, New York: Oxford University Press.

—— (1988) *The Signifying Monkey: A Theory of African-American Literary Criticism*, New York: Oxford University Press.

—— (1992) *Loose Canons: Notes on the Culture Wars*, New York: Oxford University Press.

—— (1994) *Colored People: A Memoir*, New York: Knopf.

—— (1997) *Thirteen Ways of Looking at a Black Man*, New York: Random House.

Gates, Jr., Henry Louis and Cornel West (1996) *The Future of Race*, New York: Knopf.

Geertz, Clifford (1973) *The Interpretation of Cultures: Selected Essays*, New York: Basic Books.

Gibson, Nigel (1995) 'Post-Colonial Ideological Battles', *Africa Today* 42, no. 3: 73–9.

Giddens, Anthony (1979) *Central Problems in Social Theory: Action, Structure, and Contradiction in Social Analysis*, Berkeley: University of California Press.

Gilroy, Paul (1993) *The Black Atlantic: Modernity and Double-Consciousness*, Cambridge, MA: Harvard University Press.

————— (2000a) *Against Race: Imagining Political Culture Beyond the Color Line*, Cambridge, MA: Harvard University Press.

————— (2000b) *Between Camps: Nations, Cultures and the Allure of Race*, London: Penguin.

————— (2002 [1987]) *There Ain't No Black in the Union Jack*, London: Routledge.

————— (2005) 'A New Cosmopolitanism', *Interventions: The International Journal of Postcolonial Studies* 7, no. 3: 287–92.

Glissant, Édouard (1989 [1981]) *Caribbean Discourse: Selected Essays*, translated by J. Michael Dash, Charlottesville, VA: University Press of Virginia.

————— (1997 [1990]) *Poetics of Relation*, translated by Betsy Wing, Ann Arbor, MI: University of Michigan Press.

Gooding-Williams, Robert (1996) 'Outlaw, Appiah, and Du Bois's "The Conservation of Races"', in *W. E. B. Du Bois on Race and Culture: Philosophy, Politics, and Poetics*, edited by Bernard W. Bell, Emily Grosholz, and James B. Stewart, New York: Routledge, 39–56.

————— (2009) *In the Shadow of Du Bois: Afro-Modern Political Thought in America*, Cambridge, MA: Harvard University Press.

Gordon, Lewis R. (1995) *Bad Faith and Antiblack Racism*, Amherst, NY: Humanity Books.

————— (1997) *Her Majesty's Other Children: Sketches of Racism from a Neocolonial Age*, Lanham, MD: Rowman & Littlefield.

————— (2008) *An Introduction to Africana Philosophy*, New York: Cambridge University Press.

Guha, Ranajit (2002) *History at the Limit of World-History*, New York: Columbia University Press.

Gyasi, Yaa (2016) *Homegoing: A Novel*, New York: Knopf.

Gyekye, Kwame (1995) *An Essay on African Philosophical Thought: The Akan Conceptual Scheme*, Philadelphia: Temple University Press.

—— (1997) *Tradition and Modernity: Philosophical Reflections on the African Experience*, New York: Oxford University Press.

Haley, Alex (1976) *Roots: The Saga of an American Family*, New York: Doubleday.

Hall, Stuart (1990) 'Cultural Identity and Diaspora', in *Identity: Community, Culture, Difference*, edited by Jonathan Rutherford, London: Lawrence & Wishart, 222–37.

—— (1996) 'When was "the Post-Colonial"? Thinking at the Limit', in *The Postcolonial Question: Common Skies, Divided Horizons*, edited by Iain Chambers and Lidia Curti, London: Routledge, 242–60.

—— (2016) *Cultural Studies 1983: A Theoretical History*, edited and introduced by Jennifer Daryl Slack and Lawrence Grossberg, Durham, NC: Duke University Press.

Harding, Sandra (1992) 'Rethinking Standpoint Epistemology: What is "Strong Objectivity"?', *Centennial Review* 36, no. 3: 437–70.

Hartman, Saidiya V. (1997) *Scenes of Subjection: Terror, Slavery, and Self-Making in Nineteenth-Century America*, New York: Oxford University Press.

Hegel, G. W. F. (1975 [1837]) *Lectures on the Philosophy of World History: Introduction*, translated by H. B. Nisbet, Cambridge: Cambridge University Press.

Henry, Paget (1993) 'African Philosophy in the Mirror of Logicism: A Review/Essay', *The CLR James Journal* 4, no. 1: 70–8.

Hobbes, Thomas (1996 [1651]) *Leviathan*, edited by J. C. A. Gaskin, Oxford: Oxford University Press.

Hobsbawm, Eric and Terence Ranger (eds.) (2012 [1983]) *The Invention of Tradition*, Cambridge: Cambridge University Press.

hooks, bell (Gloria Watkins) (1981) *Ain't I a Woman: Black Women and Feminism*, London: Pluto Press.

Hountondji, Paulin J. (1996 [1976]) *African Philosophy: Myth and Reality*, second edition, Bloomington, IN: Indiana University Press.

Hunt, Lynn (2007) *Inventing Human Rights: A History*, New York: W. W. Norton & Company.

—— (ed.) (1989) *The New Cultural History*, Berkeley: University of California Press.

Hurston, Zora Neale (2001) *Every Tongue Got to Confess: Negro Folk-Tales from the Gulf States*, New York: HarperCollins.

—— (2006 [1937]) *Their Eyes Were Watching God*, New York: HarperCollins.

—— (2008 [1935]) *Mules and Men*, New York: Amistad Press.

—— (2018) *Barracoon: The Story of the Last 'Black Cargo'*, New York: Amistad Press.

Inikori, Joseph E. (2002) *Africans and the Industrial Revolution in England: A Study in International Trade and Economic Development*, Cambridge: Cambridge University Press.

Irele, Abiola (1965) 'Négritude—Literature and Ideology', *Journal of Modern African Studies* 3, no. 4: 499–526.

Ivison, Duncan (2002) *Postcolonial Liberalism*, Cambridge: Cambridge University Press.

Jackson, George (1994 [1970]) *Soledad Brother: The Prison Letters of George Jackson*, Chicago: Lawrence Hill Books.

Jackson, Jr., John L. (2005a) 'A Little Black Magic', *South Atlantic Quarterly* 104, no. 3: 393–402.

——— (2005b) *Real Black: Adventures in Racial Sincerity*, Chicago: University of Chicago Press.

Jameson, Fredric (1991) *Postmodernism, or, The Cultural Logic of Late Capitalism*, Durham, NC: Duke University Press.

——— (1998) *The Cultural Turn: Selected Writings on the Postmodern, 1983–1998*, London: Verso.

Janz, Bruce B. (2009) *Philosophy in an African Place*, Lanham, MD: Lexington Books.

Jeffers, Chike (2017) 'Du Bois, Appiah, and Outlaw on Racial Identity', in *The Oxford Handbook of Philosophy and Race*, edited by Naomi Zack, New York: Oxford University Press, 204–13.

Jefferson, Thomas (1832 [1785]) *Notes on the State of Virginia*, Boston: Lilly and Wait.

Johnson, James Weldon (2015 [1912]) *The Autobiography of an Ex-Colored Man*, edited by Jacqueline Goldsby, New York: W. W. Norton.

Jones, LeRoi (Amiri Baraka) (1999 [1963]) *Blues People: Negro Music in White America*, New York: Harper Perennial.

——— (2010 [1968]) *Black Music*, New York: Akashic Books.

Kane, Cheikh Hamidou (2012 [1962]) *Ambiguous Adventure*, translated by Katherine Woods, Brooklyn, NY: Melville House Publishing.

Kant, Immanuel (1983 [1795]) *Perpetual Peace and Other Essays*, translated by Ted Humphrey, Indianapolis, IN: Hackett Publishing Company.

——— (1997 [1785]) *Groundwork of the Metaphysics of Morals*, translated and edited by Mary Gregor, Cambridge: Cambridge University Press.

Keane, Webb (2015) *Ethical Life: Its Natural and Social Histories*, Princeton: Princeton University Press.

Kendi, Ibram X. (2019) *How to Be an Antiracist*, New York: One World.

Kennedy, Dane (2005) *The Highly Civilized Man: Richard Burton and the Victorian World*, Cambridge, MA: Harvard University Press.

Ko, Dorothy (2005) *Cinderella's Sisters: A Revisionist History of Footbinding*, Berkeley: University of California Press.

Korang, Kwaku Larbi (2004) *Writing Ghana, Imagining Africa: Nation and African Modernity*, Rochester, NY: University of Rochester Press.

Laye, Camara (2007 [1953]) *L'Enfant Noir*, Paris: Plon.

Lee, Jayne Chong-Soon (1994) 'Review Essay: Navigating the Topology of Race', *Stanford Law Review* 46, no. 3: 747–80.

Lenin, Vladimir I. (1939 [1917]) *Imperialism: The Highest Stage of Capitalism*, New York: International Publishers.

Locke, Alain LeRoy (ed) (1997 [1925]) *The New Negro: Voices of the Harlem Renaissance*, New York: Touchstone.

Lorde, Audre (1984) *Sister Outsider: Essays and Speeches*, Trumansburg, NY: Crossing Press.

Lyotard, Jean-François (1984 [1979]) *The Postmodern Condition: A Report on Knowledge*, translated by Geoff Bennington and Brian Massumi. Minneapolis, MN: University of Minnesota Press.

Mamdani, Mahmood (1996) *Citizen and Subject: Contemporary Africa and the Legacy of Late Colonialism*, Princeton: Princeton University Press.

Mandela, Nelson (1994) *Long Walk to Freedom*, Boston: Little, Brown.

Matera, Marc (2015) *Black London: The Imperial Metropolis and Decolonization in the Twentieth Century*, Berkeley: University of California Press.

Mbembe, Achille (2002) 'African Modes of Self-Writing', *Public Culture* 14, no. 1: 239–73.

—— (2007) 'Afropolitanism', in *Africa Remix: Contemporary Art of a Continent*, edited by Simon Njami and Lucy Durán, Johannesburg: Jacana Media, 26–30.

McCaskie, T. C. (2003) *State and Society in Pre-Colonial Asante*, Cambridge: Cambridge University Press.

McClintock, Anne (1992) 'The Angel of Progress: Pitfalls of the Term "Postcolonialism"', *Social Text* 31/32: 84–98.

Mehta, Uday Singh (1999) *Liberalism and Empire: A Study in Nineteenth-Century British Liberal Thought*, Chicago: University of Chicago Press.

Michaels, Walter Benn (1995) *Our America: Nativism, Modernism, and Pluralism*, Durham, NC: Duke University Press.

Mill, John Stuart (1861) *Considerations on Representative Government*, London: Parker, Son, and Bourn.

—— (1869 [1859]) *On Liberty*, London: Longmans, Green, Reader and Dyer.

—— (2006 [1859]) 'A Few Words on Non-Intervention', *New England Review* 27, no. 3: 252–64.

—— (2006 [1859 and 1869]) *On Liberty and the Subjection of Women*, New York: Penguin.

—— (2015 [1859 and 1863]) *On Liberty, Utilitarianism, and Other Essays*, edited by Mark Philp and Frederick Rosen, Oxford: Oxford University Press.

Miller, Christopher L. (1990) *Theories of Africans: Francophone Literature and Anthropology in Africa*, Chicago: University of Chicago Press.

Mills, Charles W. (1997) *The Racial Contract*, Ithaca, NY: Cornell University Press.

—— (2005) '"Ideal Theory" as Ideology', *Hypatia* 20, no. 3: 165–84.

—— (2017) *Black Rights/White Wrongs: The Critique of Racial Liberalism*, New York: Oxford University Press.

Mintz, Sidney (1985) *Sweetness and Power: The Place of Sugar in Modern History*, New York: Viking Penguin.

Mintz, Sidney and Richard Price (1992 [1976]) *The Birth of African-American Culture: An Anthropological Perspective*, Boston: Beacon Press.

Moten, Fred (2017) *Black and Blur*, Durham, NC: Duke University Press.

Mphahlele, Ezekiel (1962) *The African Image*, New York: Frederick A. Praeger.

—— (1967) 'Remarks on Negritude', in *African Writing Today*, edited by Ezekiel Mphahlele, Baltimore, MD: Penguin, 247–63.

Mudimbe, V.Y. (1988) *The Invention of Africa: Gnosis, Philosophy, and the Order of Knowledge*, Bloomington, IN: Indiana University Press.

—— (1994) *The Idea of Africa*, Bloomington, IN: Indiana University Press.

Ngũgĩ wa Thiong'o (1986) *Decolonising the Mind: The Politics of Language in African Literature*, London: Heinemann.

—— (2012 [1964]) *Weep Not, Child*, New York: Penguin.

Nkrumah, Kwame (1965) *Neo-Colonialism: The Last Stage of Imperialism*, London: Thomas Nelson & Sons.

Nozick, Robert (1974) *Anarchy, State, and Utopia*, New York: Basic Books.

Nussbaum, Martha C. (1994) 'Patriotism and Cosmopolitanism', *Boston Review: A Political and Literary Forum*, 1 October. http://bostonreview.net/martha-nussbaum-patriotism-and-cosmopolitanism

―――― (2019) *The Cosmopolitan Tradition: A Noble But Flawed Ideal*, Cambridge, MA: Harvard University Press.

Nzegwu, Nkiru (1996) 'Questions of Identity and Inheritance: A Critical Review of Kwame Anthony Appiah's *In My Father's House*', *Hypatia* 11, no. 1: 175–201.

Okafor, Victor O. (1993) 'An Afrocentric Critique of Appiah's *In My Father's House*', *Journal of Black Studies* 24, no. 2: 196–212.

Oluwole, Sophie (1997) 'The Cultural Enslavement of the African Mind', in *The Essentials of African Studies*, Vol. 1, edited by Sophie Oluwole, Lagos: General African Studies Programme, University of Lagos, 129–47.

Omi, Michael and Howard Winant (1994 [1986]) *Racial Formation in the United States*, second edition, New York: Routledge.

Outlaw, Lucius (1996) '"Conserve" Races? In Defense of W. E. B. Du Bois', in *W. E. B. Du Bois on Race and Culture: Philosophy, Politics, and Poetics*, edited by Bernard W. Bell, Emily Grosholz, and James B. Stewart, New York: Routledge, 15–37.

Oyegoke, Lekan (1996) 'Leaky Mansion? Appiah's Theory of African Cultures', *Research in African Literatures* 27, no. 1: 143–48.

Oyěwùmí, Oyèrónké (1997) *The Invention of Women: Making an African Sense of Western Gender Discourses*, Minneapolis, MN: University of Minnesota Press.

Pierre, Jemima (2012) *The Predicament of Blackness: Postcolonial Ghana and the Politics of Race*, Chicago: University of Chicago Press.

Pitts, Jennifer (2005) *A Turn to Empire: The Rise of Imperial Liberalism in Britain and France*, Princeton: Princeton University Press.

Prakash, Gyan (1992) 'Postcolonial Criticism and Indian Historiography', *Social Text* 31/32: 8–19.

Quayson, Ato (2014) *Oxford Street, Accra: City Life and the Itineraries of Transnationalism*, Durham, NC: Duke University Press.

Ramazani, Jahan (2018) 'Appiah's Identities: An Introduction', *New Literary History* 49, no. 2: v–xxxix.

Ranger, Terence (2012 [1983]) 'The Invention of Tradition in Colonial Africa', in *The Invention of Tradition*, edited by Eric Hobsbawm and Terence Ranger, Cambridge: Cambridge University Press, 211–62.

Rawls, John (1971) *A Theory of Justice*, Cambridge, MA: Harvard University Press.

Richardson, Samuel (2008 [1740]) *Pamela: Or Virtue Rewarded*, edited by Thomas Keymer and Alice Wakely, Oxford: Oxford University Press.

Robbins, Bruce (2017) *The Beneficiary*, Durham, NC: Duke University Press.

Robbins, Bruce and Paulo Lemos Horta (eds.) (2017) *Cosmopolitanisms*, New York: New York University Press.

Robinson, Cedric (2000 [1983]) *Black Marxism: The Making of the Black Radical Tradition*, Chapel Hill: University of North Carolina Press.

Rousseau, Jean-Jacques (1968 [1762]) *The Social Contract*, translated by Maurice Cranston, New York: Penguin.

—— (1997 [1761]) *Julie, or The New Heloise: Letters of Two Lovers Who Live in a Small Town at the Foot of the Alps*, translated by Philip Stewart and Jean Vaché, Hanover, NH: Dartmouth College Press.

Rushdie, Salman (1981) *Midnight's Children*, New York: Knopf.

Said, Edward (1979 [1978]) *Orientalism*, New York: Vintage.

Saint, Lily (2018) *Black Cultural Life in South Africa: Reception, Apartheid, and Ethics*, Ann Arbor, MI: University of Michigan Press.

Sandel, Michael J. (1998 [1982]), *Liberalism and the Limits of Justice*, second edition, Cambridge: Cambridge University Press.

Sanders, Mark (2002) *Complicities: The Intellectual and Apartheid*, Durham, NC: Duke University Press.

Sarr, Felwine and Bénédicte Savoy, with the assistance of Isabelle Maréchal and Vincent Négri (2018) *The Restitution of African Cultural Heritage: Toward a New Relational Ethics*, translated by Drew S. Burk, Paris: Ministère de la Culture.

Sartre, Jean-Paul (1976 [1946]) *Anti-Semite and Jew: An Exploration of the Etiology of Hate*, translated by George J. Becker, New York: Schocken Books.

Schuessler, Jennifer (2017) 'Modern Language Association Moves to Reject Academic Boycott of Israel', *The New York Times*, January 7. www.nytimes.com/2017/01/07/arts/mla -reject-academic-boycott-of-israel.html

Scott, David (1999) *Refashioning Futures: Criticism After Postcoloniality*, Princeton: Princeton University Press.

Selasi, Taiye (2005) 'Bye-Bye Babar', *The Lip*, 3 March. http:// thelip.robertsharp.co.uk/?p=76

—— (2013) *Ghana Must Go: A Novel*, New York: Penguin.

Sen, Amartya (1999) *Development as Freedom*, New York: Alfred A. Knopf.

—— (2009) *The Idea of Justice*, New York: Penguin.

Serequeberhan, Tsenay (1996) 'Reflections on *In My Father's House*', *Research in African Literatures* 27, no. 1: 110–18.

Sharpe, Christina (2016) *In the Wake: On Blackness and Being*, Durham, NC: Duke University Press.

Shelby, Tommie (2005) *We Who Are Dark: The Philosophical Foundations of Black Solidarity*, Cambridge, MA: Harvard University Press.

Shohat, Ella (1992) 'Notes on the Postcolonial', *Social Text* 31/32: 99–113.

Slaughter, Joseph R. (2007) *Human Rights, Inc.: The World Novel, Narrative Form, and International Law*, New York: Fordham University Press.

Smith, Adam (1817 [1759]) *The Theory of Moral Sentiments*, Boston: Wells and Lilly.

———— (1896 [1763]) *Lectures on Justice, Police, Revenue and Arms*, Oxford: Clarendon Press.

Sollors, Werner (2018) 'Cosmopolitan Curiosity in an Open City: Notes on Reading Teju Cole by Way of Kwame Anthony Appiah', *New Literary History* 49, no. 2: 227–48.

Soyinka, Wole (1990 [1976]) *Myth, Literature and the African World*, Cambridge: Cambridge University Press.

———— (2002 [1975]) *Death and the King's Horseman*, New York: W. W. Norton.

———— (2012) *Of Africa*, New Haven: Yale University Press.

Spillers, Hortense (2003) *Black, White, and in Color: Essays on American Literature and Culture*, Chicago: University of Chicago Press.

Spivak, Gayatri Chakravorty (1988) 'Can the Subaltern Speak?', in *Marxism and the Interpretation of Culture*, edited by Cary Nelson and Lawrence Grossberg, Champaign, IL: University of Illinois Press, 271–313.

Suleri, Sara (1989) *Meatless Days*, Chicago: University of Chicago Press.

Tam, Henry (1998) *Communitarianism: A New Agenda for Politics and Citizenship*, London: Palgrave Macmillan.

Taylor, Charles (1994) *Multiculturalism: Examining the Politics of Recognition*, edited by Amy Gutmann, Princeton: Princeton University Press.

Taylor, Keeanga-Yamahtta (2016) *From #Blacklivesmatter to Black Liberation*, Chicago: Haymarket Books.

Thomas, Nicholas (1991) *Entangled Objects: Exchange, Material Culture, and Colonialism in the Pacific*, Cambridge, MA: Harvard University Press.

Thompson, E. P. (1966 [1963]) *The Making of the English Working Class*, New York: Vintage.

Toomer, Jean (2019 [1923]) *Cane*, New York: Penguin.

Trilling, Lionel (1972) *Sincerity and Authenticity*, Cambridge, MA: Harvard University Press.

Tsing, Anna Lowenhaupt (2005) *Friction: An Ethnography of Global Connection*, Princeton: Princeton University Press.

Vaihinger, Hans (1924 [1911]) *The Philosophy of 'As If': A System of the Theoretical, Practical and Religious Fictions of Mankind*, translated by C. K. Ogden, New York: Harcourt Brace.

Wallerstein, Immanuel (2004) *World-Systems Analysis: An Introduction*, Durham, NC: Duke University Press.

Walzer, Michael (1983) *Spheres of Justice: A Defense of Pluralism and Equality*, New York: Basic Books.

—— (1994) *Thick and Thin: Moral Argument at Home and Abroad*, Notre Dame, IN: Notre Dame University Press.

Weber, Max (2004 [1919]) *The Vocation Lectures: 'Science as a Vocation'; 'Politics as a Vocation'*, edited by David Owen and Tracy B. Strong, translated by Rodney Livingstone, Indianapolis, IN: Hackett Publishing.

Wilks, Ivor (1975) *Asante in the Nineteenth Century: The Structure and Evolution of a Political Order*, Cambridge: Cambridge University Press.

Williams, Eric (1994 [1944]) *Capitalism and Slavery*, Chapel Hill: University of North Carolina Press.

Wright, Richard (2014 [1940]) *Native Son*, New York: HarperCollins.

X, Malcolm and Alex Haley (1987 [1964]) *The Autobiography of Malcolm X: As Told to Alex Haley*, New York: Ballantine.

INDEX

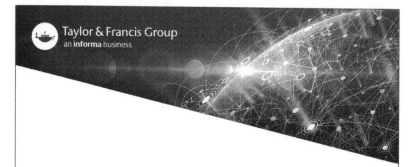